# The Byzantine Pineapple (Part 1) with Corporation X

TO GINA

COVERT!!!

REPROGRAM THE MATRIX!!

# The Byzantine Pineapple (Part 1) with Corporation X

Bill Poje

**To order additional copies of this book, contact:**
Xlibris
1-888-795-4274
www.Xlibris.com
Orders@Xlibris.com
779515

*This book is dedicated to those who share the vision...*
*and who seek to make the vision reality*

# CONTENTS

## Part 1

## What Is the Byzantine Pineapple?

## Part 2

## Example of SELP System Failures

## Part 3

## Design Parameters for Creating a New SELP System Design

# PART 1

## What Is the Byzantine Pineapple?

# How Did This Text Come into Existence?

T HIS TEXT IS the tenth revision of what was originally a fictional legal story created out of frustration to the legal challenges mounted against the (ironically named) Affordable Care Act (ACA) or Obamacare in the USA. The author is of the opinion that the legal argument approach to challenging ACA was completely misguided. The opinion of the author is that the individual mandate should have been challenged on the grounds that it creates an "existence tax" and that the framers of both the Declaration of Independence and the US Constitution would consider the imposition of any existence tax to be in direct violation of the concept of unalienable Rights to life, liberty, and the pursuit of happiness.

The author wrote revision 1. Upon reading the first draft, the author realized areas that are "legal argument flawed" based on existing Supreme Court rulings and that these issues needed to be addressed in the second revision. After creating the second revision, the author read the text and realized that this revision again had areas that are "legal argument flawed" based on existing Supreme Court rulings and that these issues needed to be addressed in the third revision. After writing and reading the third revision and coming to the same conclusion again, the author woke up from "The Matrix" and realized that there is no legal argument for independence that cannot be overruled by prior US Supreme Court rulings. In essence, the *system* is rigged against *independence*. The system is rigged against freedom of life, liberty, and the pursuit of happiness.

The system is rigged by the existence of hundreds of thousands of arcane rules and laws and regulations that are impossible for any citizen to know, yet any single one of these hundreds of thousands of arcane rules and laws and regulations can selectively be used to prosecute and persecute a citizen who falls out of favor with the state. These hundreds of thousands of arcane rules and laws and regulations comprise a Byzantine construct.

This Byzantine construct of hundreds of thousands of arcane rules and laws and regulations all end up taking capital from the citizens via taxation, fees, etc., and the capital is redistributed to those who have government influence and friends. Those on the inside eat the fruit of the Byzantine pineapple.

The solution, then, became one of following the laws of nature. In nature, there is constant change and evolution. It is time to evolve the systems of governance. The existing Byzantine pineapple system needs to evolve to the new system—a new system without a Byzantine pineapple construct.

The trick is envisioning and creating an evolution of the existing system so that the new system replaces the Byzantine pineapple system with a simpler socioeconomic legal political (SELP) system that treats citizens in a more equitable manner. The result of envisioning and creating an evolution of the existing system is this text.

# CHAPTER 1

# What Is the Byzantine Pineapple?

I T IS SAID that the definition of *insanity* is "doing the same thing over and over again, expecting a different result." It is also said that the only people you know are sane are those let out of the insane asylum because they are the only people with a certificate of sanity; you don't know about the rest of the people. Think about those two thoughts and look around you. There are plenty of insane people walking around because they keep yelling and fighting which of the right or the left is a political system that will permanently solve the issues of hunger and housing and health care for the citizens of countries.

This is not to say that the world is not in a better place because of the efforts of the right and the left. Rather, the issue is that both systems have run their course and they need an upgrade to a new system that melds the good pieces of both sides together while eliminating the corruption that dominates the current socioeconomic legal political (SELP) systems. Like the early versions of *The Matrix,* the failures of the existing SELP systems have created an escalating probability of disaster. Like *The Matrix,* there is a need to create a new SELP revision level to address the needs of the growing global human population.

There are seven-billion-plus humans on planet earth. These seven-billion-plus people are managed by 196 countries (plus odd authoritarian entities such as the United Nations or the Vatican or the Palestinian Authority). Each country/entity has its own SELP system. Each SELP system appears to have embedded system-designed corruption that will never be eliminated by adding more patchwork laws on more patchwork laws. To eliminate the corruption, there needs to be a new SELP system design. To believe otherwise fits the definition of *insanity.*

Currently, there is a large schism globally between those on the left and the right, driven by those who promote their political parties' form of SELP as a way to govern citizens. Curiously, though, there are four common social goals between not only the right and the left but also independents that really seem to cover the vast majority of political differences:

1. Provide an income to each citizen.
2. Provide health care (not health insurance) to each citizen.
3. Provide some form of housing to each citizen.
4. Treat citizens equally regardless of age or gender or race or religion or other dividing factors.

Ask yourself this question: Which political party entity has a SELP system that is known to 100 percent *cost-effectively*

1. provide an income to each citizen?
2. provide health care (not health insurance) to each citizen?
3. provide some form of housing to each citizen?
4. treat citizens equally regardless of age or gender or race or religion or other dividing factors?

The answer is *no* political party entity has a SELP system that is known to 100 percent cost-effectively accomplish the four goals outlined above. The definition of *insanity* is "doing the same thing over and over again, expecting a different result." Since the end result of following the existing parties will be the same failures to accomplish the four primary goals, why continue to follow the existing parties?

This, in a nutshell, is what *The Byzantine Pineapple* is about. The SELP systems governing humans are very *Byzantine* in nature, as every year, more and more laws are passed that increasingly make the governmental systems more and more Byzantine in nature. Annually, though, taxes are collected. Those who get the tax money are those inside the *pineapple* of government dole, while those outside the *Byzantine pineapple* get deterred by the outer defense mechanisms of the pineapple.

The text *The Byzantine Pineapple* is about a new SELP system design that restructures the existing SELP system into a new system that cost-effectively achieves four goals:

1. Provide an income to each citizen.
2. Provide health care (not health insurance) to each citizen.
3. Provide some form of housing to each citizen.
4. Treat citizens equally regardless of age or gender or race or religion or other dividing factors.

Globally, there is a growth of political independents—citizens independent from the existing political parties in their countries. More and more people globally see the political corruption going on with the existing SELP systems, and they are leaving the main political parties in droves as they seek a new SELP systems solution.

Common sense indicates to the independents that such a SELP system does not yet exist. So logically, until such a system is designed and agreed upon for implementation, the existing systems will continue to produce flawed results that will have some successes but are overwhelmingly failing because of the inherent system flaws. The inherent system flaws exist because

a. changing leadership isn't going to solve the inherent system flaws,
b. putting in term limits isn't going to solve the inherent system flaws, and
c. making governments bigger and bigger with more Byzantinely worded, massive, omnibus bills that no one is thoroughly reading before voting on is not going to solve the system flaws.

Redesigning the system to address the system flaws is necessary to solve them. But to successfully redesign and implement system reform requires first having a comprehensive SELP system plan.

The author of this text is an American. This text uses the American governmental system to present the inherent system flaws in the current

SELP systems. However, it is the opinion of the author that the same inherent flaws in the American SELP systems exist in the rest of the approximate two hundred different governmental SELP systems around the globe. There are certain common inherent SELP system construct flaws in all existing global systems that prevent achieving the four common goals.

Countries are run by either a permanent dictatorial cabal or have some form of free elections that put people into power for some length of time. No matter what system exists, there will always be some groups that must be the ruling power. This is exhibited in nature with all the various ant colonies. There is always a queen up top ruling over all the various classes in the ant colony. Someone always rules. The trick is constructing a SELP system that actually achieves the four stated SELP system goals while also establishing control over the leadership by the populace.

If a person is a citizen of a dictatorial cabal, then the citizen is subject to the whims of those in power, and the first rule of those in power is to keep power as long as possible while the events of the world change around them. If a person is a citizen of a freely elected government, then the citizen is subject to the whims of those in power too. Ergo, the way to design a new SELP system is to construct the system so that the citizens are more subject to consistent SELP system application instead of constant change based on the whims of those in power.

Regardless of the country one is a citizen of, the probability is that those in power have succeeded prior rulers / elected leaders. What occurs with the new power structure is that it creates more laws on top of all the laws that have already been established by prior power structures. These legal layers on top of decades or centuries of legal layers have created a Byzantine system.

The Byzantine system layers are like the layers of the pineapple. Inside, the Byzantine pineapple is the tasty fruit, but unless one has the machete to get at the fruit, then one does not get to partake in the feast. Only those inside get to partake of the Byzantine pineapple.

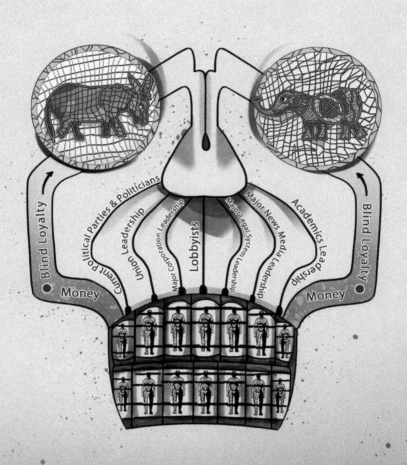

Asleep in the Matrix

*Asleep in The Matrix*
*The Daily messages sent*

Our side's slogans are coolest.
Our side is better at making fun of the other side; we are snarkier.

Our side has the plan to salvation
The other side is the path to the destruction of Earth

Our side's tax plan will solve everything
The other side's tax plan only enriches their supporters.

Our economic plan will give provide everyone with "good paying jobs"
The other side only enriches themselves while killing jobs and income.

Our health insurance plan will take care of everyone at low cost.
The other side will kill people with their plan.

Our housing plan will eliminate homelessness.
The other side will kill the homeless.

Every day is a new crisis for you to panic over.
Every new crisis needs more money to solve.

There is something wrong with you.
You are obese or too thin, too ugly or too beautiful, too dumb or too smart, etc.

You need to feel guilty about who you are and about how you are destroying the Earth.
The way to atone for your sins is to give our side more money!

Racism, Sexism, Ageism, terrorists, violent radicals, etc., are everywhere.
Hate and distrust everyone….especially "the other side."

The other side is "racist".
Our side is not "racist."

There are not enough laws.
More and more and more and more laws are always needed.

Passing massive omnibus bills that no one is reading at the threat of government shutdown is just good politics.
There is no other way.

The government mess is all because of the other side.
Our side is virginal.

You are either 100% with our side or you are the problem.
There is no other way.

# CHAPTER 2

# About the Author

T HE READERS WILL undoubtedly ask themselves at some point, What qualifies the author to be believed for a new SELP system design? The answer is that the author has both education and experience, qualifying him to be able to opine on the subject with validity. A small sample of a lifetime of work and learning is noted below.

From the fall of 1984 to the spring of 1988, the author completed 115 undergraduate school hours and sixty graduate school credit hours. In essence, the author completed both undergraduate and graduate school in four years' time.

The undergraduate degree was a joint accounting / business administration degree and an MBA that was conferred in the concentration of finance and operations management. Between undergraduate and graduate schools, the author completed twenty hours of information systems coursework (enough for a minor) as well as completing or auditing all coursework required for an MBA concentration in marketing.

During graduate school, the author took international finance and economics taught by Dewey Daane, who was appointed to the Board of Governors of the Federal Reserve Board by John F. Kennedy in November 1963 and served on the board until 1974. Mr. Daane was instrumental in the ending of the Bretton Woods Agreement that established the gold standard. When Wall Street crashed in 1987, the *Wall Street Journal* immediately had a front-page article by Mr. Daane, concerning the latest ongoing market crash.

The author spent eight years working for a global Japanese manufacturing firm that produces both automotive and nonautomotive products. The author was responsible for managing the standard cost system and all governmental regulatory reporting in terms of NAFTA, AALA, CAFE, and product marking and labeling.

The author was also in charge of product estimating. The author was instrumental in changing an annually financial-losing company for nineteen out of twenty years into an annually profitable corporation. The products estimated were primarily push-pull cables (e.g., transmission cables, brake cables, and steering cables). And the author was responsible for at least 25 percent of all original equipment manufacturing push-pull cables sold annually in the USA.

The author also lived in both Grand Cayman and Grand Bahama Islands during which time the author was the financial controller for the largest exporter out of the Bahamas. The author installed a full ERP / accounting system, financial report writer, payroll system, biometric time and attendance system while also cleaning up the corporation's financials. The author also envisioned, designed, and started implementation of a now fully functional data system that collects data from the Bahamian manufacturing facilities' PLCs (for a factory that operates 24-7-365 or never-ceasing operations) and transfers the data to the ERP / accounting system as well as to management.

The author has accomplished a lot more and has a variety of products that have been successfully market-tested and are ready for global production. The author is of the opinion that this lifetime of accomplishment qualifies him to design a new SELP system.

CHAPTER 3

# How Do Current Socioeconomic Legal Political (SELP) Systems Work?

WITH RESPECT TO SELP systems in the USA and many other countries around the globe, there are elections, and the election winning regime does the following:

1. Pass a bunch of laws, adding laws on existing laws.
2. Cut or raise taxes.
3. Cut or add social welfare programs.

Obviously, there are foreign policy issues and other issues that also occur, but for the most part, these actions occur. These are three established reasons why the SELP systems will ultimately fail:

1. The continuous stream of new laws enacted continually add Byzantine layers to existing Byzantine SELP systems that have basically made all citizens illegal in some way, shape, or form just by the citizens leading their normal lives, while also making criminal activities legal.

What eventually ends up occurring is a breakdown of law because the common citizens see lots of common citizens that they feel they should be free from being incarcerated and having their lives ruined unnecessarily due to ambiguous application of laws. Simultaneously, the common citizens see many powerful people commit what they feel are obvious crimes, and the powerful people go free. For the citizenship, the philosophical construct of what is legal and illegal is gone.

2.  All the tax changes every year create an unstable, disruptive system that has no endgame and no real purpose. However, all the tax changes establish and pit different classes of citizens against one another rather than treating all citizens equally.

    What ends up occurring is that all sorts of arcane taxes are continually created with rules designed to benefit certain parts of the populace at the expense of other parts of the populace. But since the taxation system is so convoluted, the citizenship really can't tell what is truly going on with taxes. All the common citizens know is that there are base tax rates and tax credits and base income deductions, but there is no way for them to have any confidence that they are being treated equitably in relationship to others. This leads to a belief on the part of much of the common citizenship—that they are getting screwed as their tax dollars are unfairly given to others.

3.  All the social welfare programs exist to spend tax dollars while never existing for an endgame. However, all the social welfare programs establish and pit different classes of citizens against one another rather than treating all citizens equally.

    What ends up occurring is that the social welfare programs rarely cease. Instead, they continue to grow in size to be paid more, and there will be more government employees to manage the programs while providing less benefit to the common taxpaying citizenship. This leads to class anger between those paying for the social welfare programs and those receiving from the social welfare programs.

The above three issues establish the parameters for a new SELP system:

1.  A system design that clearly defines for all citizens what is conceptually legal and illegal
2.  A system design that has a stable tax system that treats citizens equally.
3.  A system design of social welfare programs that is streamlined and treats all citizens equally

# CHAPTER 4

# The Structure of the Text

T*HE BYZANTINE PINEAPPLE* is intended to be a simplistic presentation of a new SELP system and specifically a macroeconomic formula that is a more equitable government management system that can be ultimately understood by high school-–educated people globally. The opinion is that common people will get it once the plan is presented to them. The opinion is that once people get it, they will support the plan.

Current political parties and politicians, union leadership, major corporation leadership, lobbyists, major legal system leadership, major news media leadership, and academics leadership won't like the plan. Why? Because the Byzantine system that they have created enriches those at the top of these echelons at the expense of the common populace while also perpetuating their power grasp over the common populace.

These echelons won't state their objection so bluntly. They will proclaim that the SELP system proposals in this text and, specifically, the macroeconomic flat tax formula contained herein are worthless because some universities and federal agencies haven't developed and blessed the SELP system proposals backed up by arcane mathematical formulations understood by only a few. Ask yourself this question: If the echelons really know what they proclaim to know, then why are all the current SELP systems continuously such a jumbled mess?

The fact of the matter is that the echelons are all enriching themselves at the expense of the common populace because of the current Byzantine SELP systems that they created and perpetuated! Follow the Benjamins. The echelons get paid to perpetuate the current SELP systems.

This text is Part 1 of 3 planned texts:

1.  This version of *The Byzantine Pineapple* Part 1 has 2 parts. An abridged version is also available. The Abridged Version only contains the first half noted below. This version is the low cost version for mass consumption.

    The first half deals with Systems Analysis and Systems Design of the existing SELP systems. The Systems Design segment presents a brand new Flat Tax Macroeconomic formula that can be used at any level of government and by any government on the planet.

    The second half of the text presents the Corporation X Business Plan. This plan is a 10 year $6 billion dollar global sales vision that creates products as well as a production and marketing corporation that can be used to take The Byzantine Pineapple to the Common People around the globe…while greatly profiting those who choose to invest in Corporation X.

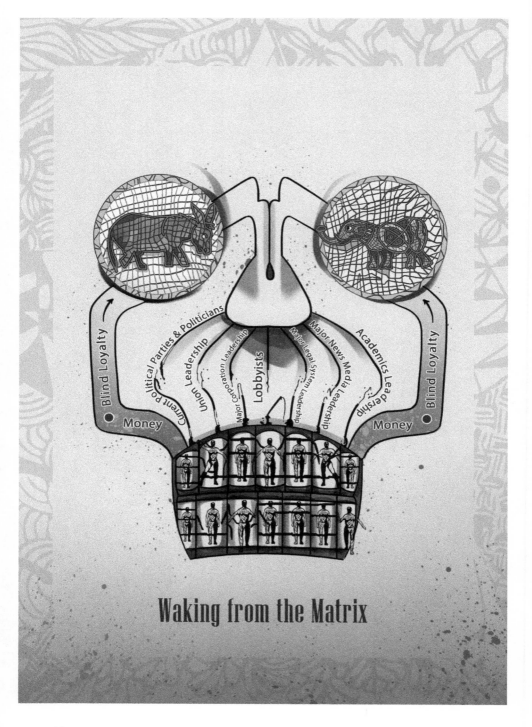

**Waking from the Matrix**

Our side's slogans are coolest.

Our side is better at making fun of the other side; we are snarkier.

**SLOGAN'S AND MAKING FUN OF PEOPLE ARE NOT PLANS IMPROVING SOCIETY!**

Our side has the plan to salvation

The other side is the path to the destruction of Earth

**NEITHER SIDE HAS A CLEARLY DEFINED PLAN FOR THE FUTURE!**

Our side's tax plan will solve everything

The other side's tax plan only enriches their supporters.

**BOTH SIDES ALWAYS MODIFY TAXES TO BUY VOTES!**

Our economic plan will give provide everyone with "good paying jobs"

The other side only enriches themselves while killing jobs and income.

**THERE 70,000,000+ UNEMPLOYED PEOPLE IN THE USA.**
**IT IS IMPOSSIBLE TO CREATE 70,000,000+ JOBS!**

Our health insurance plan will take care of everyone at low cost.

The other side will kill people with their plan.

**INSURANCE SYSTEMS ARE COSTLY AND TREAT PEOPLE UNEQUALLY.**
**IF "HEALTH CARE" IS A RIGHT OF ALL CITIZENS THEN THERE IS NO NEED FOR A HEALTH INSURANCE SYSTEM!**

Our housing plan will eliminate homelessness.

The other side will kill the homeless.

**NEITHER SIDE HAS A VIABLE PLAN TO ELIMINATE HOMELESSNESS!**

Every day is a new crisis for you to panic over.

Every new crisis needs more money to solve.

**THE STORIES OF CRISIS ARE BEING PLANTED TO GET MONEY!**
**THERE IS NO GREAT CRISIS!**

There is something wrong with you.

You are obese or too thin, too ugly or too beautiful, too dumb or too smart, etc.

**JUST BECAUSE WE ARE ALL DIFFERENT DOESN'T MEAN THERE IS SOMETHING WRONG WITH YOU!**
**YOU ARE WHO YOU ARE...AND NO DRUGS/PRODUCTS/ETC. WILL CHANGE THAT!**

~~You need to feel guilty about who you are and about how you are destroying the Earth.~~

~~The way to atone for your sins is to give our side more money!~~

JUST BECAUSE SOMEONE CLAIMS THEIR CHARITY/CAUSE IS DOING "GOOD" DOESN'T MEAN THAT IT IS.

QUIT FEELING GUILTY BECAUSE SOME ECHELON TELLS YOU TO FEEL GUILT!


~~Racism, Sexism, Ageism, terrorists, violent radicals, etc., are everywhere.~~

~~Hate and distrust everyone…..especially "the other side."~~

IF YOU ADD UP ALL THE REPORTED ACTS OF HATE IN THE USA IT ADDS UP TO 0.0000000% OF THE 300+ MILLION PEOPLE IN THE USA!

THAT MEANS THAT 300+ MILLION OF US CITIZENS GET ALONG WELL EVERY SINGLE DAY!


~~The other side is "racist".~~

~~Our side is not "racist."~~

RACISM MEANS MAKING DECISIONS BY RACE!

THE BIGGEST RACISTS ARE THE POLITICAL PARTIES, GOVERNMENTS, MAJOR CORPORATIONS, NEWS MEDIA AND EDUCATIONAL INSTUTUTIONS! WHY?

BECAUSE THEY SEGREGATE AND MAKE DECISIONS BASED SOLELY UPON RACE!


~~There are not enough laws.~~

~~More and more and more and more laws are always needed.~~

ALL CITIZENS ARE NOW ILLEGAL BECAUSE THERE ARE SO MANY LAWS NOW THAT IT IS IMPOSSIBLE NOT TO BE ILLEGAL.

LESS, BETTER DEFINED LAWS ARE NEEDED!


~~Passing massive omnibus bills that no one is reading at the threat of government shutdown is just good politics.~~

~~There is no other way.~~

MASSIVE LEGISLATION WRITTEN BY LOBBYISTS AND PASSED WITHOUT ANYONE REALLY READING THE BILLS WRITTEN SO VAGUELY THAT THE COURT SYSTEM MUST CONTINUALLY RULE UPON THE VAGUE LEGISLATION SHOULD BE LABELED AS "CRIMINBUS BILLS."

THERE ARE OTHER WAYS.


~~The government mess is all because of the other side.~~

~~Our side is virginal.~~

BOTH SIDES HAVE CREATED THE MESS OF GOVERNMENT!

BOTH SIDES ARE RESPONSIBLE!


~~You are either 100% with our side or you are the problem.~~

~~There is no other way.~~

BLIND ADHERENCE TO FALSE PROMISES OF POLITICAL PARTIES IS THE PROBLEM!

THERE ARE OTHER WAYS!

# PART 2

# Example of SELP System Failures

# CHAPTER 5

# Legal Systems
# Who or What Is Legal, and
# How Is Legality Determined?

IN THE USA, it is seemingly impossible to determine what actions are criminal or not criminal. This is because there is no clear definition of what determines what is legal and what is illegal. To explain this further, the author chooses to tie together four seemingly independent legal examples:

1. Troubled Asset Relief Program (TARP)
2. Affordable Care Act (ACA a.k.a. Obamacare) vis-à-vis the Congressional Budget Office (CBO)
3. Personal-choice freedom: legal/illegal substances as well as vices and seat belts
4. Civil asset forfeiture and economic eminent domain

## *Troubled Asset Relief Program (TARP)*

TARP was developed to bail out a variety of companies that stood to enter bankruptcy due to a combination of fraud and just plain bad decision-making. All of a sudden, seemingly overnight, both the Republicans and the Democrats proclaimed that the USA and other countries around the globe *must* pass the bailouts. Otherwise, there would be a global economic crash.

Obviously, these declarations were made without the politicians or the news media even reading or comprehending the very open-ended TARP legislation. The Matrix program told the politicians and the news media to tell citizens that TARP *must* happen, and they repeated what they were told to repeat. It was amazing how the news media and the politicians all said the same thing every day. It was almost like they all received a daily email telling everyone how to speak and act in front of the cameras.

This bailout was sold as what could only be described as trickle-down socialism. The social benefit of bailing out the corrupt corporation- or government-created regulatory system would be of greater social benefit versus letting the bankruptcy courts take over and settle things.

What really happened with TARP was that a bunch of very wealthy and powerful people (and their entourages) stood to lose massive amounts of wealth due to their bad money management decisions. They didn't want to do that. So they cooked up a scheme like that of *Chicken Little*'s "The sky is falling" with their paid-for politicians and media to proclaim that they must be bailed out or the economic system would collapse and the four horsemen of the economic apocalypse would ride the land. So the wealthy and powerful got their losses paid for by the governments that work for them. They didn't end up losing money (and, inherently, power).

And then to help pay for TARP, interest rates were lowered to 0 percent so the banks could borrow at 0 percent and lend at higher rates, guaranteeing positive cash flow. And the corporations were gifted tax credits to benefit the newly appointed White House–selected ownership. How convenient!

Who pays for this scheme? *Taxpayers!* This magic TARP legislation seemingly appeared overnight and put the taxpayers on the hook for the losses. Even better for the rich and powerful, the whole scheme was legal because ruling governments around the globe said it was legal. The issues that global governments saying that TARP's legal doesn't mean that TARP wasn't criminal.

## Affordable Care Act (ACA a.k.a. Obamacare) vis-à-vis the Congressional Budget Office (CBO)

Soon after TARP, the USA passed the ACA, even though, obviously, no politicians or news media actually read the legislation. To pass the legislation, the politicians had the legislation financially scored by the Congressional Budget Office (CBO) as being deficit neutral with all sorts of other hokey proclamations about how many Americans would now be insured due to ACA. Using a little common sense, one can understand just how hokey the ACA sales job by the CBO was.

After the passage of ACA, there was subsequent rules and regulations issued. There is no one definitive source that can state how many regulations were attributable to ACA, but the number appears to be between five thousand and fifteen thousand rules and regulations issued. Each rule and regulation had a cost impact associated with it.

Ask yourself this question: How could the CBO have scored the cost impact of all the subsequent five-thousand-plus rules and regulations that came out after ACA passed? The answer is that there is no way CBO could have scored the cost impact of all the added rules and regulations!

This demonstrates how ludicrous the current SELP is while also epitomizing the Byzantine pineapple. This is a Byzantine system of government bureaucracies passing unread legislation using known phony numbers to justify passing the unread legislation—legislation that creates more and more Byzantine layers of government, as well as law, rules, and regulations.

Make sure you understand what this means! This means that the CBO is useless. It 100 percent fails at the task it was created to achieve. Yet simultaneously, the CBO scoring is a major lynchpin of passing legislation (Legislation being voted into law that few, if any, politicians have read and understand) in the United States! The political parties have created a system whereby useless proclamations are used to justify passing legislation! In the private industry, that is considered fraud. In the political industry, it is all legal to commit such fraud!

At the same time, there is now an *existence tax* on the citizen's head. If the citizen *exists*, the citizen is now subjected to a health insurance tax just for existing. If the citizen doesn't either pay directly for health insurance or pay a tax, then the citizen is a *criminal* (!).

Ask yourself this question: Do you think an existence tax is what the signers of the Declaration of Independence had in mind when they established the freedom to pursue life, liberty, and happiness? The author certainly doesn't and is of the opinion that the vast majority of citizens of countries around the globe agree.

## Personal-Choice Freedom: Legal/Illegal Substances as well as Vices and Seat Belts

Simultaneously, the surveillance technology of the US government has grown by leaps and bounds. The citizen basically has to assume that every single action or word uttered is being recorded somewhere and can be used against them at any point in time.

The failure is that as human history has shown, humans like to engage in vices and personally dangerous behavior, and the legal system has outlawed the personal activity that people like to engage in while letting others get away with the same behavior because under some form of logic, one form of the same behavior is legal and the other is illegal. This allows the all-surveilling state unfettered reign to lock up and besmirch selective lives without really a concept of what being a criminal is. *The Trial* has begun.

This means that many citizens can't truly enjoy freedom of personal choice—a.k.a. life, liberty, and the pursuit of happiness—because the all-surveilling state has constructed a SELP system with selective prosecution. It is the selective prosecution that drives wedges into society because citizens find themselves at war with the state over issues of what being a criminal is.

There are five primary categories that need a SELP resolution, because no matter whether the activities are legal or illegal, there will always be millions of citizens engaging in the categories. A certain percentage of citizens will always partake in

1. using recreational substance of all sorts of natural and synthetic products,
2. trading money for sexual activity,
3. gambling,
4. engaging in personally dangerous physical activity for a thrill, and
5. aborting.

There has never been a time in recorded human history where a percentage of the human population hasn't engaged in the five behaviors above. Whether it offends one's personal morals or not, people are going to engage in these behaviors. Why is the SELP system structured to ruin people's lives by criminalizing them for being human?

Why is it criminal for the common citizens to be jailed for their vices, to be denied employment for their vices, and to have degrading marks put by the government on their personal records when the rich and powerful rarely get convicted for the same behavior? Look at the population of jailed drug offenders in the USA, and it is obvious that more common citizens are being jailed versus wealthy citizens.

Why is it illegal for common citizens to enjoy some vices while it is legal for those controlling the politicians and media to get a TARP-sized bailout? The bailouts occurred because the rich and powerful were too busy enjoying their vices rather than managing their investments.

It is only illegal for one and legal for the other because of the hypocritical way the SELP system is designed. Changing the existing SELP system is the only way to allow citizens to truly enjoy life, liberty, and the pursuit of happiness as the citizen sees fit versus as proscribed by those in power.

The alternative is to keep doing the same thing over and over again, expecting a different result. The hypocritical SELP construct is like an earlier version of the Matrix, and it is inevitable that eventually, the system will fail. The failure will occur when the twenty-trillion-dollar (and exponentially growing) US federal government debt bubble bursts.

Don't you think that the US federal government debt bubble will burst? Ask yourself this question: What do the 1929 crash and the S&L crisis in the 1970s, the crash of 1987, the dot-com crash of 2000, the Enron crash, and the combo subprime loan and fraudulent bond marketing crash all have in common? The answer is that the government and financial leaders all thought the same thing you are thinking now: It will never happen. None of them ever saw it coming!

## Civil Asset Forfeiture and Economic Eminent Domain

First, the state made illegal, noninjuring-to-others activities that humans like to choose to do, thereby making virtually all citizens illegal. Then the state developed 24-7-365 monitoring of citizens so that all the activities of humans are monitored for selective prosecution of noninjuring-to-others activities. What's left? Appropriating for the state the assets of those not directly tied into the state.

Civil asset forfeiture was created to take the ill-gotten gains of big drug lords who pay no income taxes and who made their money illegally. Now the laws are being used to confiscate cars and other properties of citizens who are mostly trying to just live the life of a human.

Eminent domain is a legal concept that allows governments to take a citizen's property for the public good, such as for building a road or a sewer system. Now the legal concept has been expanded to "economic eminent domain" whereby the trickle-down socialism of the new economic development outweighs the personal property rights of the citizen.

In both cases, the same overall concept occurs: the government takes the personal property of the citizen and the citizen has no recourse, except through expensive court-related expenses that also consume the citizen's life.

Those inside the Byzantine pineapple gain, and those outside lose out. And whether morally right or wrong, it is all legal!

# Tying the Four Concepts Together

In the USA, a citizen can watch an X Games athlete attempt jumping a motorcycle forty-seven feet into the air for a vault, and that is legal for the X Games athlete to do. Or a citizen can watch people play football and see physical contact that can and does cause injury, and that is legal to do.

However, if a citizen drives a vehicle without wearing a seat belt, they can be fined or imprisoned for their personal choice because driving without wearing a seat belt is dangerous and, therefore, is illegal. And since the vehicle was used in the commission of a crime, the state can simply take the vehicle, and the citizen is screwed.

For just the top 10 prescription drugs in the USA, there are 150 million monthly prescriptions. Those are prescriptions and not the number of pills sold.

For the top 100 prescription drugs in the USA, the total amount of monthly prescriptions probably exceeds the number of citizens in the USA. Those are prescriptions and not the number of prescription pills actually sold. And those are just prescribed drugs and not over-the-counter drugs. And that doesn't include illegal drug use!

Common sense should tell one that with all the prescribed OTC and illegal drugs sold in the USA, just about every single person in the USA is drugged up on something. Common sense also should tell one that whether a drug is considered legal or illegal, it is irrelevant to individuals either responsibly or irresponsibly using the drug. It is a matter of choice.

The point is that the overall behavior of engaging in thrill-seeking or in using recreational drugs is no different behavior than the behavior followed by those who use legal drugs or those who engage in dangerous sporting activities. However, while the behavior is the same, the legality/illegality of the behavior is defined differently. Ask yourself this question: Do you really know why that is?

If a citizen gambles with their money, it used to be illegal virtually everywhere. Now there are more legal gambling options, but it is still illegal in most localities for private citizens to gamble with their money.

Gambling is a matter of placing a bet and taking the risk that the bet will pay off. This is considered illegal in localities based on a concept of moral behavior.

If a citizen puts money into the financial markets, the citizen is, in effect, gambling. The citizen is placing a bet that the financial reward of the investment will outweigh the risk that the bet will pay off. The theoretical concept is that if the stock collapses or interest rates change, the investor bears the risk and reaps the reward. Somehow, this is considered moral behavior, while gambling is considered immoral, even though the bottom-line behavior is the same.

At the same time, the politicians can rob the populace through taxation structured in a Byzantine manner that selectively rewards a few while harming others. This is what happened with TARP. The legislative, administrative, and judicial branches all agreed to cover the losses of the gamblers who placed losing bets on financial instruments. The three branches of the US government (and many other governments, which followed suit on TARP) claimed that it is legal to take taxpayer's money and bail out wealthy donors who stood to lose fortunes on bad bets. The three branches of the US government (and many other governments, which followed suit on TARP) placed their own bet that the trickle-down socialism effect would do less harm to society versus letting the bankruptcy system run its course.

The question is, Why are select gambling behaviors *legal* and other select gambling behaviors *illegal*? The answer is that the SELP system in place is structured to keep it that way.

This current SELP system is doomed to fail. Why? The potential for abuse is obvious, and the stories of system abuse continue to grow annually. Citizens are being taxed at ever-increasing rates while they see that the benefits of the ever-increasing taxation are not being delivered. Instead, the citizens see

1. ever-increasing layers of laws that are only complicating their lives, doing things like making the citizen a criminal if he disagrees with the now-instituted existence tax;

2. regulatory taxation unnecessarily increasing the citizen's cost of living;
3. criminal behavior being declared noncriminal for those with money and power by the three branches of government; and
4. common citizenship being increasingly incarcerated or having stains on their police record, which affect the ability to find gainful employment, for the same behavior being declared noncriminal for those with money and power.

This simplistic presentation points out why the class of independents is growing both in the USA and also globally. It is patently obvious to the citizens that the political parties are on the take and really don't have a plan in place to address what the citizens see as the root cause of the breakdown of the concept of law. The common people are moving away from the political parties, leaving only the hard-core political party acolytes in the political parties. The hard-core acolytes are now in control of the political parties, while the independents seek a new SELP system to address the flaws of the existing SELP systems. The problem the growing independents have is that there is currently no plan presented to the citizens for a new SELP system that they feel they can support!

To create a new SELP system that will actually achieve the originally stated four goals, one must understand why the current SELP economic systems fail to achieve the stated four goals. The explanation of why the SELP systems are doomed to fail economically is illustrated by the analysis of the taxation systems in place as well as the analysis of the inherent flaws of the needs-based welfare systems.

# CHAPTER 6

# Why Existing SELP Systems Are Doomed to Fail

THE SEEDS OF failure for the existing global SELP systems were sown a long time ago. It is only because of the greatly increased human population, coupled with modern technology, that the seeds sown have fully manifested themselves.

The inequities of the existing SELP systems used to be able to be buried because there were less people to manage and humans couldn't see the big picture. However, with so many people today, it is impossible for the ruling party to buy votes with corruption like they used to because there are too many votes to out-and-out buy. Also, those getting screwed by the corruption can see it occur in real time, and the ability to play back what has been said is educating people to the lies that have been told.

Until the governmental macroeconomic structure goes through an evolution that is simplified and treats citizens equally, these will be the situations prevalent today: hate-filled diatribe and clever slogans spewed back and forth between the right and the left, which may score political points and make for entertaining television. But the diatribe does nothing to solve the fundamental structural deficiencies of the existing SELP systems. Until there is a fundamental restructuring of the governmental macroeconomic structure, the current existing SELP system failures will not go away.

To create a new SELP system design for the governmental macroeconomic structure, there must be systems analysis of the existing SELP governmental macroeconomic structure first to understand why the existing failures exist. Following are analyses of the failures of the taxation system and needs-based systems.

## Taxation System Failures

*Death* and *taxes* are stated to be the only certainties of human existence. With respect to taxes, the phrase never states that taxes are intelligently applied.

In the year 2014, the government of France advocated a 75 percent tax rate on select entities. The United Nations is advocating increased taxation in various manners. The United States government has increased taxation over the last few years. Around the globe, there is a Tea Party movement that advocates less taxes and less government. In every country, there are always a variety of taxation system changes made by those in power. Ask yourself this question: Why should any human believe that any of these changes will create a better way for the citizens of the country?

The answer is that *no one* should believe that any taxation changes will have the desired effect unless there is a provable method that the tax changes will work. The failure with the current SELP taxation systems in place and proposed to be changed is that the systems are based entirely on what University of Chicago economics professor Frank Wright termed as unknown unknowns.

University of Chicago economist Frank Wright coined a concept called unknown unknowns. This concept explains the failure of the various tax rates and the various governmental budgets that are put forth as being necessary for the management of humans. The calculations of both the tax rates and the budgets are based on economic theorems that are based on economic *unknown unknowns*. These economic unknown unknowns ultimately doom the implementation of the tax rates and budgets to systematic failure. This is epitomized in art by Neo saying to Agent Smith in the climax of the Matrix trilogy: "It was inevitable."

Let's look at some examples of this inevitability of economic unknown unknowns. The United States government issues a ten-year budget annually. This budget is based on assumptions that are unknown.

There are assumptions like

1. what the interest rate of debt issued and retired will be for each of the ten years,
2. what the annual inflation rate that occurs will be for each of the ten years,
3. what the unemployment rate that occurs will be for each of the ten years,
4. what the tax rates in effect will be for each of the ten years,
5. what the social security payments made will be for each of the ten years, and
6. what will the GNP be for each of the next ten years.

The list can continue, but the point is that each of these factors is an *unknown*. The assumptions are known, but these assumptions are known to be false. The actual rates of each of the budgetary factors are unknown unknowns. The factor details are unknown, and the future factor details are unknown. Everything is an economic unknown unknown. The failure of the governmental taxation system and, inherently, the governmental budget is inevitable.

Recent years have seen the emergence of new economic theories, such as economic theories that mathematically *prove* that negative interest rates are how governments should operate. In other words, instead of entities earning interest on money lent to the government, the entities are better off losing money lent to governments. Instead of there being a positive time value of money, there is a negative time value of money.

Citizens are told to accept these economic theories issued by those who have mathematical formulations and positions of power and the backing of powerful people to support the economic theory. The failure is that the economic theorems behind such mathematical formulations are based entirely on escalating economic unknown unknowns. The mathematical theory works on paper because the paper theory assumes away all economic unknown unknowns as not fitting the formula. Therefore, the formula is not wrong. It is the economic unknown unknowns that are wrong!

The failure is that the economic unknown unknowns are the reality of SELP existence. The proper economic formula for a new SELP design seeks to eliminate economic unknown unknowns via the logical construction of the formula instead of assuming away the economic unknown unknowns. By applying systems analysis and systems design to the construction of a macroeconomic formula, a simpler, more powerful macroeconomic formula for taxation and government can be created.

## The Inherent Flaws of Needs-Based Social Welfare Programs

Governments have tons of social welfare programs. These social welfare programs are almost exclusively needs-based systems.

Needs-based systems are ultimately doomed to fail. This failure is evidenced by the following programmatic events that occur with respect to needs-based systems:

1. A needs-based system requires adding Byzantine layers of bureaucracy, which adds cost and inefficiencies in operation of the needs-based systems.
2. Citizens are not treated equally by needs-based systems. The needs-based system segregates citizens into different categories, rewarding some citizens at the expense of others.
3. The categories-sorting method of the needs-based system is ultimately modified over time. This modification process adds more Byzantine layers to the original needs-based system categorization process.
4. By their very nature, needs-based systems are not designed to eliminate needs. Needs-based systems perpetually require

a continuously morphing Byzantine decision rules set to continuously make decisions about needs as the political parties in charge of the governmental systems change over time. The system is therefore about perpetuation of the needs-based systems rather than needs elimination.

5. Needs-based systems do not provide 100 percent quality control. They always have the following:

A. User fraud of individuals or cartels who seek to profit from submitting false data to receive the capital being distributed by the needs-based system.

B. Political, capital/largesse fraud. Political parties manipulate needs-based systems for internal fraud as well as to both buy votes and repay political favors to donors of the political parties.

C. Natural system error. Any individual's needs change over time, but the systems design of needs-based systems is not prepared to track and account for changes in the needs / lack of needs of hundreds of millions (let alone billions) of citizens. The simplest example is the needy person who wins the big capital lottery. An income-based needs system is prone to not recognize that the lottery winner theoretically no longer has a need because of a suddenly large asset base.

D. Conflicting needs-based systems that do not account for citizens' actions as a whole with respect to the variety of needs-based systems that a government has created. Each individual needs-based system is actually a subsystem to a macroeconomic total system. The more individual subsystems are in place, the more subsystems a citizen can apply to for needs-based assistance. The more subsystems are in place, the more Byzantine the decision-making process becomes to track the citizen. The more each individual needs-based subsystem morphs over time, the more the tracking subsystems for each needs-based subsystem must morph over time to account for all the changes that have occurred. This epitomizes the Byzantine pineapple. As time moves forward, the systems become more Byzantine.

Ask yourself this question: What is sought to be accomplished by all the various needs-based systems that governments create? The answer needs to be defined in clear, specific terms rather than nebulous buzzwords.

This system's analyst perceives that the needs-based systems are what people also termed as social welfare systems. The terminology is irrelevant. What are relevant are the goals to be accomplished. At the very simplistic core, there are three basic goals that are sought by governmental needs-based systems / social welfare systems:

1. Ensure that all citizens have enough capital to exist on a daily basis.
2. Ensure that all citizens are provided basic health care. (Note: health care is not health insurance.)
3. Ensure that all citizens have an address to call home, which has the basic needs necessary for survival (heat, power, and basic appliances).

It really is that simple. Those three items really are what the majority of government programs seek to accomplish.

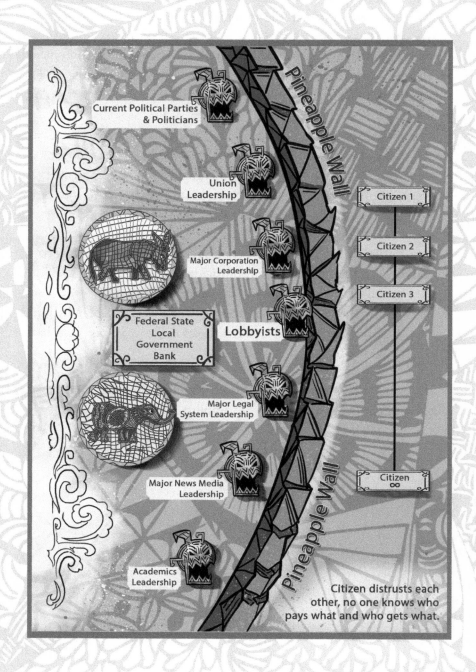

Current Political Parties & Politicians

Union Leadership

Major Corporation Leadership

Federal State Local Government Bank

Lobbyists

Major Legal System Leadership

Major News Media Leadership

Academics Leadership

Pineapple Wall

Pineapple Wall

Citizen 1

Citizen 2

Citizen 3

Citizen ∞

Citizen distrusts each other, no one knows who pays what and who gets what.

# PART 3

## Design Parameters for Creating a New SELP System Design

# CHAPTER 7

# Defining Design Parameters for a New SELP System Design

TO CREATE A new SELP system, one must first establish parameters to use in establishing a new SELP system. Think about it: if one cannot clearly state the parameters of a new SELP system, then how can one know whether the desired results of a SELP System are achieved?

The following is a list of design parameters for creating a new SELP system design:

1. Use information systems' systems analysis and systems design techniques for problem-solving.
2. Eliminate as many economic unknown unknowns as possible.
3. Establish 100 percent quality control.
4. Treat citizens equally regardless of age, gender, race, ethnicity, income level, asset base, location, religion, or any other demographic factor normally used to divide citizens of a nation.
5. Establish the "keep it simple and stupid" principle (KISS principle) wherever possible.
6. Eliminate (over time) all current government social welfare programs/systems and replace them with a system that addresses the primary four goals established in the introduction.
7. Tie government spending to government revenue.

The explanations of these design parameters for creating a new SELP system design are as follows:

1. *Use information systems' systems analysis and systems design techniques for problem-solving.*

Designing a new SELP system design is similar to a new information system. Designing information system is all about problem-solving. Ask yourself this question: How is a problem defined? If the problem cannot be properly defined, then the systems analysis and systems design required to solve the problem cannot be applied. However, this concept of defining the problem applies to problems as they exist on a daily basis.

The author of this text grew up in a household with a parent who continuously responded to daily stimuli by exclaiming "The world is full of problems!" or "The government is full of problems!" or "There are so many problems in the world today!" and an ad nauseam amount of ways of stating the same thing. The author experienced in life wherein other people walking around, saying "That child is a problem child" or "That person is a problem employee." The author has been beset by such stimuli, such as "Capitalism is such a problem," "Socialism is a problem," "Communism is a problem," etc. Other expressions extend to ethnic terms such as the Jewish problem, the Palestinian problem, etc. Religion is also used in this context: "Catholics are a problem" or "Islam is a problem" or on and on and on.

The entire problem statements above are actually meaningless statements because there is no tangible definition of the word *problem*. Unless the problem in each case can be defined in a tangible method, then the statements are meaningless. Ask yourself this question: How many times during the next seven days will I hear the word *problem* used, and how many times will there be a clear definition of what the *problem* actually is? Better yet, how many times in the next seven days will you hear politicians and media personalities use the word *problem* without stating any clear problem analysis or problem solution design?

Information systems' systems analysis and systems design define the term *problem* as "a gap between reality and the way that things are desired to be." Bridging the gap is the implementation plan.

This explains why current SELP systems fail with respect to legislation passed. There is never a clear definition of systems analysis, systems design, and implementation process defined with legislation passed. Instead, what is passed is cobbled together. Another set of laws is on top of other laws with no clear definition of what *problem* the new legislation is actually trying to solve!

Try reading the Affordable Care Act or other omnibus bills passed by the United States Congress and signed by the president of the United States of America. There can be no wonder why it takes a supreme court to rule on what is actually being stated in the legislative acts. The texts are convoluted and ill-defined.

The evidence that no true systems analysis and systems design work is performed on legislation can be seen with actions regarding the passage and initial attempt to repeal and replace ACA. The passage of ACA had a "cornhusker kickback" and a "Louisiana purchase," as well as a subsequent stack of regulations ten feet high. The initial ACA repeal and replace had an "Alaska purchase." If a legislative act is organized via systems analysis and systems design, then there would be no state buyouts for votes or subsequent massive regulation stack. Proper systems design that treats citizens equally would never have bribes for votes, nor would there be a need for massive subsequent regulations. The original legislation would already contain the regulations required.

The politicians and the academics declare loudly that "This is politics!" The politicians and the academics declare loudly that there is no better SELP system that can be created. Wake up from "The Matrix"! Don't fall for that Jedi mind trick! A better SELP system can be designed and implemented. What is required is to take a comprehensive view of the existing system and then designing the new system to address existing system flaws. The differences between the two models are the implementation path.

2.  *Eliminate as many economic unknown unknowns as possible.*

    Part 1 already documented what economic unknown unknowns are. The issue is whether the reader really understands what the impact of existing unknown unknowns baked into the existing SELP systems are and whether the reader understands how these unknown unknowns can be eliminated.

    Think about this: Each year for ten years, leading up to 2009 and 2010, the US federal budget made all sorts of projections comprised of thousands of pages of unknown unknowns. Then in 2009 and 2010, the US government passed TARP, ACA, and a nearly trillion-dollar stimulus package. Logically, this means that all projections made for the prior ten years leading up to 2009 and 2010 were essentially junk. The budgets didn't account for the massive spending of these programs!

    Similarly, the budgets of 2009 and 2010 and in subsequent years ended up being junk. Those budgets were based on expected results of the legislation of TARP, ACA, and a nearly trillion-dollar stimulus package passed, but those expectations were actually unknown unknowns that never came to fruition.

    This process of governments passing useless budgets based on unknown unknowns–based projections occurs annually at every level of government in each governing authority around the globe. These budgets are essentially junk because they will never come close to being a reality.

The definition of *insanity* is "doing the same thing over and over again, expecting a different result." Continuing to create and pass junk budgets over and over again and expecting problems to be resolved is insane.

3.  *Establish 100 percent quality control.*

    After World War II, an American statistician named William Edward Deming went to Japan to assist in the industrial reconstruction of Japan. The Deming Prize that carries his name is such a prestigious award that Japanese television annually broadcasts the award presentation.

    Dr. Deming would hold seminars on quality control where statistical analysis of errors would be calculated via a simple example. A bowl full of mostly white but with scattered red balls would be brought forth. A paddle would be inserted into the bowl, and the seminar attendees would mathematically calculate the error rate of production as noted by the amount of red (error) balls withdrawn from the bowl.

    After a series of calculations that mathematically prove the error rate, Dr. Deming would, in essence, inform the seminar attendees that they have wasted their time. The reason that the time is wasted is that for all the mathematical calculations performed, not one single step has been taken to prevent red balls from entering the bowl. The errors still occur.

    The needs-based systems in place are all designed to *inject* red balls into the system. Continuing to use flawed needs-based systems while expecting these systems to work to solve problems is insane.

    In other words, it is a waste of time to design a system that allows for quality defects and then spend time documenting the error rate. The inherent system problems are *not* being solved. Hence, 100 percent quality control is a design parameter of a new SELP system.

4. *Treat citizens equally regardless of age, gender, race, ethnicity, income level, asset base, location, religion, or any other demographic factor normally used to divide citizens of a nation.*

The United States of America's Declaration of Independence states, "We hold these truths to be self-evident, that all men [people] are created equal, that they are endowed by their Creator with certain unalienable Rights, that among these are Life, Liberty and the Pursuit of Happiness."

This statement contains a parameter of systems design. The parameter is a systems design that treats people equally while allowing for life, liberty, and the pursuit of happiness.

One of the biggest contributors to hate is distrust. One of the greatest sowers of distrust is the existing SELP systems. This is because the existing SELP systems establish parameters of treating citizens differently depending on who the citizen is. Rather than treating citizens equally because the citizens are citizens with equal rights, the existing SELP systems segregate citizens into thousands of different classes and then allot government resources based on the thousands of different classes established by the government.

What is the result of all the subclassifying of the citizenship? Distrust, because those who pay more and get less of the Byzantine pineapple dole or who perceive they pay more and get less distrust the government and those receiving more and paying less or who are perceived to be receiving more and paying less. Those actually paying less and receiving more also don't want the gravy train to end, and they promote distrust by deflecting citizens to other perceived injustices except the ones that they themselves are committing.

The purpose of the government shouldn't be segregating and pitting the citizenship against one another. The purpose of the government should be to treat the citizenship equally.

5. *Establish the "keep it simple and stupid" principle (KISS principle) wherever possible.*

Currently in the United States, there is a constant push to pass more and more laws via massive omnibus bills that aren't really being read or debated before being voted upon. This epitomizes how the US government is operating in an anti-KISS-principle manner.

The new SELP system needs to reestablish a simpler citizen-to-government relationship. This can be done by defining a simpler database relationship of citizen to government. There should be no need for each government department to have multiple databases carrying redundant citizen data. Instead, there should be a single department of information systems that feeds the functions of government, thereby simplifying the citizen-to-government relationship.

6. *Eliminate (over time) all current government social welfare programs/systems and replace them with a system that addresses the four primary goals established in the introduction.*

As already noted in the text, there are hundreds of US federal government needs-based programs all designed to actually accomplish three primary tasks:

1. Provide an income to each citizen.
2. Provide health care (not health insurance) to each citizen.
3. Provide some form of housing to each citizen.

Also, already noted is that needs-based programs are doomed to never accomplish the stated program goals due to inherent system flaws. Ergo, a new SELP system needs to eliminate (in an orderly methodical manner over time) existing needs-based systems and replace these systems with simpler KISS-adhering programs.

4. *Tie government spending to government revenue.*

The only way to stop current politicians from sending future generations further in debt is to construct a SELP system that balances government spending to government revenue. It's called living within your means.

There is another aspect to think about. For the United States federal government (and many other federal governments around the globe), no political parties have a macroeconomic plan that balances government revenue to government spending. Inherently, this means that none of the political parties really value this idea.

# CHAPTER 8

# A New SELP System Design

T HE NEW SELP macroeconomic system that meets the goals and parameters are defined herein.

The following is a construct of a new SELP systems design that fits the parameters previously outlined:

A.  Use tax subrates to prebudget government departments.
B.  Sum up the tax rates to come to a flat tax rate applied to all citizens.
C.  Force all benefits for government workers to a 401(k)-style plan.
D.  Eliminate all health insurance (over time) and just have the government pay for the citizens' health-care bills out of a new health-care tax subrate.
E.  Eliminate all government programs (over time) that pay anything for citizens based on need. Establish a new monthly payment for all citizens with the same monthly government stipend regardless of any factors, such as age, race, asset base, income level, etc. The stipend is established by a new stipend tax subrate.
F.  Eliminate all government housing programs (over time). Establish government housing areas where any citizens can go live if they so desire. The zones are paid for by a new tax subrate.

The following text expands upon these system design parameters:

A. *Use tax subrates to prebudget government departments.*

Ask yourself this question: Why *must* governments be funded by forms of appropriation bills? The answer is that there is no *must*. How government departments are funded is a matter of choice.

The failure of existing SELP systems—a failure that has been proven again and again throughout history—is that without spending control on those in power, they will continue to increase taxes and government spending to the point of bankrupting the country. The way to accomplish control is to prebudget government with taxation that is directly tied to government spending.

The way to prebudget government via taxation is to use tax subrates for each government department. This is best illustrated for understanding by using a direct example.

The following page contains the US federal budget for 2013 as per Wikipedia. The second page shows each department's budgeted percentage as a percentage of the PTD. Whether these pages ended up being the exact budget is irrelevant for the purposes of illustration. The total percentage of department is listed as well as the total percentage of all spending that each department accounts for.

The totals column is ultimately a percentage of the total annual population of tax dollars (PTD). Assume that the PTD for the US federal budget for 2013 was $9 trillion. The military's budget of $672.9 billion for the year was 7.3 percent of the PTD. Therefore, the subrate for the military is 7.3 percent.

Applying the same logic to all the US governmental departments provides the result on page 49.

http://en.wikipedia.org/wiki/2013_United_States_federal_budget

| Agency | Discretionary | Mandatory | Total | % of Total |
|---|---|---|---|---|
| Department of Defense including Overseas Contingency Operations | 666 | 6.7 | 672.9 | 17.7% |
| Department of Health and Human Services including Medicare and Medicaid | 80.6 | 860.3 | 940.9 | 24.7% |
| Department of Education | 67.7 | 4.2 | 71.9 | 1.9% |
| Department of Veterans Affairs | 60.4 | 79.4 | 139.7 | 3.7% |
| Department of Housing and Urban Development | 41.1 | 5.2 | 46.3 | 1.2% |
| Department of State and Other International Programs | 56.1 | 3.4 | 59.5 | 1.6% |
| Department of Homeland Security | 54.9 | 0.5 | 55.4 | 1.5% |
| Department of Energy | 35.6 | −0.6 | 35.0 | 0.9% |
| Department of Justice | 23.9 | 12.7 | 36.5 | 1.0% |
| Department of Agriculture | 26.8 | 127.7 | 154.5 | 4.1% |
| National Aeronautics and Space Administration | 17.8 | −0.02 | 17.8 | 0.5% |
| National Intelligence Program | 52.6 | 0 | 52.6 | 1.4% |
| Department of Transportation | 24.0 | 74.5 | 98.5 | 2.6% |
| Department of the Treasury | 14.1 | 96.2 | 110.3 | 2.9% |
| Department of the Interior | 12.3 | 1.2 | 13.5 | 0.4% |
| Department of Labor | 13.2 | 88.4 | 101.7 | 2.7% |
| Social Security Administration | 11.7 | 871.0 | 882.7 | 23.2% |
| Department of Commerce | 9.5 | −0.5 | 9.0 | 0.2% |
| Army Corps of Engineers Civil Works | 8.2 | −0.007 | 8.2 | 0.2% |
| Environmental Protection Agency | 9.2 | −0.2 | 8.9 | 0.2% |
| National Science Foundation | 7.4 | 0.2 | 7.5 | 0.2% |
| Small Business Administration | 1.4 | −0.006 | 1.4 | 0.0% |
| Corporation for National and Community Service | 1.1 | 0.007 | 1.1 | 0.0% |
| Net interest | 0 | 246 | 246 | 6.5% |
| Disaster costs | 2 | 0 | 2 | 0.0% |
| Other spending | 34.0- | 61.7 | 29.5 | 0.8% |
| **Total** | **1,264** | **2,539** | **3,803** | |

M% is defined as the % of PTD dedicated to fund military = $672.9B — 7.3%

E% is defined as the % of PTD dedicated to fund education = $72B — 0.80%

VA% is defined as the % of PTD dedicated to fund Veteran Affairs = $140B — 1.55%

ST% is defined as the % of PTD dedicated to fund the State Department = $60B — 0.66%

DHS% is defined as the % of PTD dedicated to fund the Department of Homeland Security = $56B — 0.62%

EY% is defined as the % of PTD dedicated to fund the Energy Department = $56B — 0.62%

J% is defined as the % of PTD dedicated to fund the Justice Department = $37B — 0.41%

A% is defined as the % of PTD dedicated to fund agriculture = $154B — 1.71%

N% is defined as the % of PTD dedicated to fund NASA = $18B — 0.20%

NIP% is defined as the % of PTD dedicated to fund the National Intelligence Program = $52B — 0.58%

T% is defined as the % of PTD dedicated to fund transportation = $98B — 1.08%

TRE% is defined as the % of PTD dedicated to fund the Department of Treasury = $110B — 1.22%

INTER% is defined as the % of PTD dedicated to Fund the Department of Interior = $13.5B — 0.15%

LBR% is defined as the % of PTD dedicated to fund the Department of Labor = $102B — 1.13%

CE% is defined as the % of PTD dedicated to fund the Commerce Department = $9B     0.10%

ACE% is defined as the % of PTD dedicated to fund the Army Corps Engineers = $8B     0.09%

EPA % is defined as the % of PTD dedicated to fund the EPA = $9B     0.10%

CNS% is defined as the % of PTD dedicated to fund the National Science Foundation = $8B     0.09%

SB% is defined as the % of PTD dedicated to fund the Small Business ADM = $1.4B     0.01%

NSF% is defined as the % of PTD dedicated to fund the Corp. for Nat'l Service = $1.1B     0.01%

IS% is defined as the % of PTD dedicated to fund a proposed Department of Information Systems = TBD

Total All Subrates     18.43%

This 18.43 percent is the basis for a flat tax. However, there are more items to be addressed, namely, needs-based programs, which also tie back to government department budgeting.

With respect to a government department budget, there are four categories of expenditures:

1. Current labor obligations (payroll, payroll taxes, 401(k), etc.)
2. Future labor obligations (pension, disability, etc.)
3. Operations expenses
4. Capital program expenses

Items 1, 3, and 4 can be fixed in value, which makes these expenditures *known*. It is the second category of future labor obligations that is an *unknown unknown*. By grandfathering out all future labor obligations to be handled in a different manner, the budgets for the departments shrink. The way to handle the future labor operations moving forward is resolved by the way that current needs-based programs are grandfathered out and replaced with a much simpler system. How this is accomplished is explained as the text proceeds.

B. *Force all benefits for government workers to a 401(k)-style plan.*

Pension plans are 100 percent unknown unknowns. The *401(k)* plans are known. The unknown unknown needs to be 100 percent replaced with the known for *all* government employees.

C. *Eliminate all health insurance (over time) and have the government pay citizens' health-care bills out of a new health-care tax subrate.*

Insurance is a product of pooled risk to pay out a benefit if an incident occurs. But if the public opinion and direction is that all citizens are provided health care, then why is there a need for health insurance?

Another way of phrasing this is that if citizens are mandated to buy health insurance plans that do not cover 100 percent of the possible medical issues that a citizen may need health care for, then there is no 100 percent quality control. If the goal is to provide health care yet the mandated insurance doesn't cover the expenses of the health care required, then what use is the health insurance?

The fact is that there actually is no need for a health insurance system for citizens. The expenditures can be billed to and paid for by the federal government. This dramatically brings costs down because all the systems required to support Byzantine payment and remittance systems, as well as paying large salary amounts to an eliminated industry, will be eliminated.

The phase in plan would be to start with dental services. A definition of the annual services (such as annual teeth cleaning) as well as the base-covered cost for dental procedures is required. For example, if a citizen destroys his/her teeth because he/she is a crystal meth user, then the citizen gets a new set of base teeth to provide health care to the citizen. If the citizen is capable of affording and wants a better set of replacement teeth, then the citizen can pay the difference between the base set and the final set.

Using such a system to start would allow the bugs to be worked out of such a system, and then the system can be expanded to cancer treatments, AIDS treatments, etc. Eventually, a stasis occurs, and all citizens have 100 percent health care.

With respect to the government departments' future benefits for medical, there simply is no need for department budgets to carry the costs. The medical insurance costs (and administrative costs) would also disappear from the corporate world, increasing profits and allowing for a greater PTD annually. All medical cost bankruptcies would vanish over time.

Using the 2013 health and human services budget as a proxy, the expenditure is $940 billion. This works out to a 10.44 percent value for a subrate labeled $H$ percent.

D. *Eliminate all government programs (over time) that pay anything for citizens based on need. Establish a new equal monthly payment to all citizens. The stipend is established by a new stipend tax subrate.*

Common sense dictates that all citizens need capital to survive. But as the text has already shown, the needs-based system of allocating capital to citizens is flawed. How to replace the needs-based systems with a system that achieves the stated SELP system goals of treating citizens equally as well as following the KISS principle is the question.

The solution is to establish a tax subrate that gathers funds that are redistributed monthly to citizens in an equal amount regardless of age, race, gender, income, asset base, or any other factor. The monthly amount distributed to each citizen will not be a significant amount but will be enough to live off because of the following:

A. As the prior section noted, the citizen will not be subjected to expenses related to health care.
B. As the subsequent section notes, a tax subrate to provide paid-for living to any citizen who desires it can be established.

Without anyone having to pay for health or shelter expenses, a citizen can exist on a nominal stipend each month. Other citizens also know that when an individual or family is seeking assistance, the basic needs of the individual or family are already taken care of.

Inherently, this means grandfathering out the Social Security System because a citizen can always decide to save or not to save for the future, but that is a moot point. The citizen's needs are taken care of monthly in a KISS-principle manner.

This also means the elimination of the unemployment tax system as well as many other federal systems. Since citizens are already receiving a monthly stipend and can receive health care and can move into a housing zone if necessary, then there is no need for mass quantities of disparate government programs.

The concept of "too big to fail" is no longer relevant. If a corporation fails and citizens lose jobs, that is a tragedy. But the needs of the citizens are automatically covered, so there is no need for government involvement in performing trickle-down socialism to prop up failing corporations.

Assume that there are three hundred million citizens and the target value sought is to redistribute $1 trillion annually. This works out to $278/month to each citizen or approximately $65/week. Based on a $9 trillion PTD, this works out to a flat tax rate of 11.11 percent.

Those in larger cities will argue that such an equal distribution is unfair to them because the cost of living in their locality is greater. This is a false argument because of the following:

1. If it is possible to define the locations of the greater economic costs, it is possible to define the government(s) in charge of the greater economic cost.
2. There is nothing precluding the region/government(s) of the greater economic area from also collecting and redistributing local income in the same manner to the local citizens, thereby supplementing the federal stipend.

In other words, any difference in economic value is a local issue. It is the role of the federal government to treat citizens equally.

The payment system for each citizen can be established and managed by a new federal department of information systems. To qualify for a monthly benefit, citizens must annually certify their existence in person with the new federal department of information systems. At the same time, such items as voter registration can also be taken care of, thereby eliminating the perpetual angst over the registered voter issue.

C. *Eliminate all government housing programs (over time). Establish government housing areas where any citizen can go live if the citizen so desires. The zones are paid for by a new tax subrate.*

If citizens want a place to live, they can't just go into the wilderness and build their own home from scratch. There are too many humans on earth, and all the properties are owned by some entity. The choices are to own or to rent or to live free with others, or else, some other accommodations are made.

Current SELP systems have evolved systems to provide housing to the needy, but the same issues that plague all need-based systems are built into the existing SELP systems. The existing systems are too costly as well as fraud filled.

The KISS system solution is that the government must provide basic housing with basic utilities to any citizen who wants to exist in such a basic lifestyle. The government pays the utility and maintenance costs, and the payment for such housing is paid for out of another tax subrate to pay for the housing.

The federal allocation per citizen should be in an equal amount per person. If localities feel that the local economics require more funding per citizen, then, as with the monthly stipend, the local government for a defined area can supplement the federal payment.

Other Subrates Required to Balance Out the US Model

There are three other subrates required for the US model:

A. A factor to balance out the grandfathering out of the existing Social Security System. The theory is that the Social Security System should balance itself out. The reality is probably something different, and this points out the flaws inherent in the existing Social Security System.
B. A factor for paying the annual interest amount due for the national debt.
C. A factor for paying down at least some of the national debt principal.

# The Base Macroeconomic Formula

The summation macroeconomic formula of the flat tax plan is the following:

Flat Tax Rate % = (S%) + (SS%) + (H%) + (L%) + (D%) + (I%) + (M%) + (E%) + (VA%) + (ST%) + (DHS%) + (EY%) + (J%) + (A%) + (N%) + (NIP%) + (T%) + (TRE%) + (INTER%) + (LBR%) + (CE%) + (ACE%) + (EPA%) + (NSF%) + (SB%) + (CNS%) + (IS%)

Note: The full definitions of each % is in appendix A on page 67.

Using the already noted percentages, the calculated rate is as follows:

Flat Tax Rate % = (11.11%) + (0%) + (10.44%) + (5.55%) + (TBD) + (2.73%) + (7.3%) + (.80%) + (1.55%) + (0.66%) + (0.62%) + (0.62%) + (0.41%) + (1.71%) + (0.2%) + (0.58%) + (1.08%) + (1.22%) + (0.15%) + (1.13%) + (0.10%) + (0.09%) + (0.10%) + (0.09%) + (0.01%) + (0.01%) + (TBD%) = 48.26% plus TBD

While this amount seems excessive, the final actual rate should be less than the value shown in this model. Why? There are three reasons:

1. Incomes rise as existing costs are eliminated so the percentage of population of tax dollars required for the same funding level decreases.
2. There is existing taxation that will vanish.
3. Citizens can change the rates.

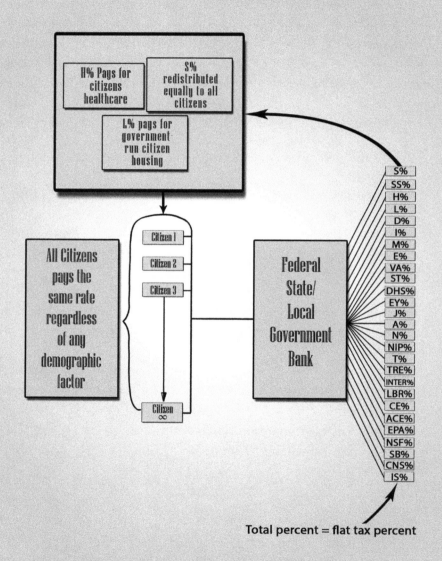

Citizen trust each other because
they know everyone is treated equally.

H% Pays for citizens healthcare

S% redistributed equally to all citizens

L% pays for government-run citizen housing

All Citizens pays the same rate regardless of any demographic factor

Citizen 1
Citizen 2
Citizen 3
Citizen ∞

Federal State/ Local Government Bank

S%
SS%
H%
L%
D%
I%
M%
E%
VA%
ST%
DHS%
EY%
J%
A%
N%
NIP%
T%
TRE%
INTER%
LBR%
CE%
ACE%
EPA%
NSF%
SB%
CNS%
IS%

Total percent = flat tax percent

*Incomes rise as existing costs are eliminated so the percentage of population of tax dollars required for the same funding level decreases.*

The operations of corporations become more profitable due to the elimination of the medical costs from corporations. The direct expense (paying health insurance premiums) and indirect experience (staff, legal, etc.) to support the HR systems will vanish over time as the plan is implemented.

Assume that this is a 10 percent increase in the PTD. This increases PTD from $9 trillion to $9.9 trillion. Under the $9 trillion example, the rate is 48.26 percent in the hypothetical model equal to $4.34 trillion in taxes collected. If the PTD is now $9.9 trillion, then the aggregate required to fund the same $4.34 trillion is now 43.87 percent for a 4.39 percent decrease.

A 20 percent PTD increase would drop the rate to 40.22 percent for an 8.04 percent reduction.

## *There is existing taxation that will vanish.*

There is no accounting in the model for taxation that disappears. The following list is just a few of the major explanations of what that statement means:

1.  There is no longer an unemployment system and unemployment taxation. The expense of such a system will disappear (lowering the departmental taxation rate subrate), and paychecks will increase as citizens are no longer paying this tax.
2.  Corporate expenses are lessened as the massive amount of human resource work required for medical insurance disappears as the direct health-care system is built and insurance is phased out. Profits are up, which means there is more income to be taxed.
3.  With the elimination of the health insurance system over time, the expenses for medical should drop. All the money paid to support a complex Byzantine insurance system simply vanish by

a simpler, more streamlined system. Also, employee paychecks increase because federal insurance system taxes are eliminated.

4. Since the federal government is prebudgeted, then spending pork barrel via buying votes to pass an appropriation bill goes away. The legislative branch can't get money for programs by holding spending bills hostage for pork barrel projects to buy the votes of the politicians.

5. The current focus of government departments is to spend 100 percent of the current year budget so that the next year will see an increase in budget money to spend. Prebudgeting the government means that there now becomes a focus to more effectively use the budgetary dollars available, because when the current year's funding runs out, then the department is shut down until the next year. Plus, capital purchases for a department must be planned out, so there is now a need to build a departmental cash reserve to be able to invest in major new projects.

6. All the tax dollars spent to support various special interests are minimized because there is simply no need for the government to spend money on the special interests. Since all citizens have no immediate financial need for base-living expense or medical or housing, then there is no need to have government money spent on stimulus, jobs programs, etc. The responsibility shifts away from the current trickle-down socialism construct to a free-market construct.

These are but a few of the anticipated tax reductions of a simpler flat tax system that ties government spending to government revenue via a fixed tax subrate system. The point is that the final rate can be expected to be a lot less than the 48 percent calculated using the existing budgets.

## Citizens can change the rates.

A method of citizen-approved rate changes must be built into the SELP system. System evolution must be built into the system construct.

Consider how this SELP system would function versus the existing United States system. Currently, every time the military wants a new program or some special interest wants more money to fight for a cause, then funding is achieved by an act of congress. This process is lumped together with other funding requests in the bill, and eventually, enough votes are cobbled together for approval. There is no real accountability for what eventually happens.

With the subrate system described, the US military gets 7.3 percent. If the military wants a new program, then the funding is either achievable within the 7.3 percent or the funding isn't achievable. If the military makes the case that the 7.3 percent is not enough to fund current operations while also planning for future programs, then the military can petition to have the rate changed to a higher rate. The issue is that there is now an emphasis on future planning within the context of a fixed budgetary amount.

In the case of a new military operation à la desert storm or desert swarm, the military can either afford the operations within the context of the 7.3 percent or the military can petition the citizens for a new tax subrate that is designed to pay for the operation. This new subrate provides visibility to the citizens that this specific subrate of the flat tax is funding the operation, and as the operation winds down, the subrate should reduce and disappear.

The same logic is true for events such as the next Ebola or Zika or other scares plastered across news media that are used to argue that more money is needed to combat the scary, new potential pandemic. Either the funding is already available or an added subrate is needed.

Obviously, the primary subrate for a department can be broken down further. Continuing the example, the 7.3 percent for the US military can be broken down further into US Army, Air Force, Navy, Marines, Coast Guard, and what other designations required to sum up to the 7.3 percent.

The following are other benefits to society by this form of SELP system:

A. The angst in society over homeless or medical bankruptcies or other social issues goes away because there is a "100 percent coverage for all the citizens of the country." When citizens see panhandlers, they can know with 100 percent assuredness that there is no direct reason for the panhandlers to be seeking money.

B. Every week and every month, there is hoopla over government reports about jobs and unemployment. While the reporting will still go on, the hoopla will go away because there is simply no need for it. Who cares how many people are employed? The issue is that citizens are 100 percent taken care of for the basics of life.

C. Citizens know where their tax dollars are going versus the current fungible system where money appropriated for one purpose is suddenly used for a completely different purpose.

D. For situations such as violence against women, there is a clearly defined residence where the woman can go and live.

E. For convicts released from prison, there is a clearly defined place to live and an income to exist off. This can minimize crime as society will be less tolerant for thieving, so there is no need for thieving.

F. Social diseases such as sexually transmitted diseases should be easier to treat and control. Why? Because there are no financial or administrative procedural issues other than proof of citizenship to getting both diagnosis and treatment.

There are a plethora of other benefits, such as a simplified KISS principle, that the SELP system should provide. The concept is that the citizenship is working together toward a common SELP structure that any citizen in the modern world should be able to rapidly understand.

# THE CHOICE IS ALWAYS YOURS TO MAKE!

| BYZANTINE SYSTEM | SIMPLIFIED SYSTEM |
|---|---|
| A SYSTEM BASED UPON UNKNOWN UNKNOWNS | A SYSTEM BASED UPON KNOWNS |
| BIAS BASED SYSTEM | EQUALITY BASED SYSTEM |
| CONTINUOUS CRISIS SYSTEM | PLANNED PLACID SYSTEM |
| SYSTEM THAT PROMOTES FRAUD OPPORTUNITIES | SYSTEM MINIMIZING FRAUD |
| SYSTEM THAT CREATES FEDERAL DEFICITS | SYSTEM BALANCING THE BUDGET |
| SYSTEM THAT NEVER SOLVES CITIZEN NEEDS FOR A) PERSONAL INCOME B) HEALTH CARE C) ADDRESSING HOMELESSNESS | SYSTEM COVERING ALL 3 NEEDS 100% |
| SYSTEM THAT PROMOTES VIOLENCE & HATRED | SYSTEM PROMOTING PEACE AND EQUALITY |

# CHAPTER 9

# Conclusion

THE SELP SYSTEM described in this text are as follows:

1. It is not an "overnight" solution. Implementation requires the populace to buy off that this solution is to be implemented over a multiyear period.
2. It treats all citizens equally regardless of any demographic factors, such as age, race, religion, ethnicity, etc.
3. It places importance upon being a citizen and requires that all humans within a country, either a citizen or else, have some form of SELP system designation (work visa and others). The benefits provided to noncitizens depend on the SELP system designation of the noncitizen.
4. It provides for 100 percent coverage of all citizens' basic needs of food, shelter, and health care.
5. It is designed for a nonviolent transition from existing SELP systems to this new SELP system.

Some people will cry "This is Socialism!" Look back at the current US budgets %'s documented in this text. The Military only accounts for 7.3% of the budget. The rest of the 92.7% is arguably going to fund Socialism! The money is already being spent. It just isn't being spent in an equitable and cost effective manner.

Ask yourself this question the next time you hear a politician or a news pundit speaking about legislation proposed to solve some societal problem: Will the legislation cost-effectively deliver 100 percent coverage for the citizens as described by the SELP system described in this text?

The author of this text can state with 100 percent certainty that unless the legislation is actually designed as described in this text, the legislation will fail. Some parties inside the Byzantine pineapple reap the benefits, and those outside the Byzantine pineapple get the shaft.

The definition of *insanity* is "performing the same actions over and over and over again, expecting a different result." To abscond with a marketing phrase and a movie tagline used in the past, it is time to stop the insanity and to wake up from "The Matrix"!

To show your support for *The Byzantine Pineapple* please visit www.poje.biz and sign up for the Quarterly Corporation X Newsletter. The more people who sign up because they see the concepts proposed the greater the power to build the New Construct!

# APPENDIX A:

# Definitions of the Flat Tax Formula

## Economic Unknown Unknowns of the Flat Tax Formula

S% is defined as the percentage of PTD dedicated to fund a universally equal redistribution of wealth to all citizens.

SS% is defined as the percentage of PTD required to resolve all current outstanding Social Security obligations as the system is phased out. In theory, this should be 0 percent for the program is designed to pay for itself.

H% is defined as the percentage of PTD required for health care of citizens.

L% is defined as the percentage of PTD dedicated to paying for living quarters for citizens who opt for the public housing zone option.

## Economic Knowns of the Flat Tax Formula

I% is defined as the percentage of PTD required to make interest payments on the US debt.

D% is defined as the percentage of PTD required to pay down a portion of the US debt.

M% is defined as the percentage of PTD used to fund the military department.

E% is defined as the percentage of PTD dedicated to fund education.

VA% is defined as the percentage of PTD dedicated to fund Veteran Affairs.

ST% is defined as the percentage of PTD dedicated to fund the State Department.

DHS% is defined as the percentage of PTD dedicated to fund the Department of Homeland Security.

EY% is defined as the percentage of PTD dedicated to fund the Department of Energy.

J% is defined as the percentage of PTD dedicated to fund the Justice Department.

A% is defined as the percentage of PTD dedicated to fund agriculture.

N% is defined as the percentage of PTD dedicated to fund NASA.

NIP% is defined as the percentage of PTD dedicated to fund National Intelligence Program.

T% is defined as the percentage of PTD dedicated to fund transportation.

TRE% is defined as the percentage of PTD dedicated to fund the Department of Treasury.

INTER% is defined as the percentage of PTD dedicated to fund the Department of Interior.

LBR% is defined as the percentage of PTD dedicated to fund the Department of Labor.

CE% is defined as the percentage of PTD dedicated to the Commerce Department.

ACE% is defined as the percentage of PTD dedicated to fund the Army Corps of Engineers.

INTER% is defined as the percentage of PTD dedicated to fund the Department of Interior.

EPA% is defined as the percentage of PTD dedicated to fund the Environmental Protection Agency.

NSF% is defined as the percentage of PTD dedicated to fund the National Science Foundation.

SB% is defined as the percentage of PTD dedicated to fund the Small Business Administration.

CNS% is defined as the percentage of PTD dedicated to fund the Corps for National Service.

IS% is defined as the percentage of PTD dedicated to fund the Department of Information Systems.

*HUMOROUSLY* **GRAPHIC!**
*VERY* **NOVEL!**

# CONTENTS

# INTRODUCTION

CORPORATION X IS a six-billion-dollar, ten-year global sales plan (see page 78). The plan is for a marketing and production company to produce and market initially the works of Bill Poje as books, films, and merchandise. The lead product is *Painless*— the first story in the Less trilogy (*Blindless, Timeless*). Other products include *UnManifest Destiny, The Salvador Dali Cypher, Party Late* (a musical based on Senator Smilfme Smarmy stories), *H & Job, NLM, Subprime, Mom's Amazing Journey, Eye See You. Know the N.O. No, The Worst and the Dumbest, The Old Ones, A Day on the Life,* three other movie remakes, two Shakespeare remakes, collected short stories and essays, and many more, as well as *The Byzantine Pineapple*.

This presentation of the business plan is both for entertainment as well as a business plan presentation. Hence, a stodgy "there is only one way to present business plans" person will abhor the presentation, while the person of good nature may find humor in the presentation. Humor is important in entertainment, and if the author is incapable of humoring the reader, then how can the reader expect that the author can humor people globally?

This business plan is not filled with numbers, such as projected ROI or IRR. There is no specific "we will sell *X* quantity" annually. Instead, this is more of a big-picture-thinking presentation. If you are an experienced businessperson or investor or even just a common human and you see the big picture, then you will know that there is very good profit to be made. All it takes is a little brainpower.

The chapter headings are titled with *plan* for each functional department of a corporation. Some may argue that *plan* is too kind of a word for chapters 4–8 since a limited amount of detail is presented, especially when compared to the first three chapters. However, the details for the support departments aren't necessary to present in great detail. The big money is in the first three chapters. The other departments support the primary actions necessary to move Corporation X forward.

The Corporation X plan started in 2007 when the author was living in Grand Cayman and Grand Bahama while employed as the financial controller for the largest exporter out of the Bahamas, for an organization as big as a planned *Painless* movie production. Many events happened, such as going through or evacuating from nine hurricanes in three years, which changed the planned futures of many people. The author had a personal choice of what to do for the future: stick with island life throughout the Caribbean (sigh) or move on to the next phase of life. But what would that phase be?

The author walked into a movie theater and watched yet another annual big-budget, big-name movie that sucked. The light went on, and he said, "I can *and* will do better than this crap." Hence, the vision started.

Since then, the author has self-funded to create the published books, as well as test-marketing the products with phenomenal success. The author has also built the business plan while self-learning the industry, as well as making certain key contacts. The author also takes the time to be the primary caregiver to his now ninety-three-year-old mother. The time has now come to move everything forward to the next phase.

The Corporation X business plan is extremely flexible. Different investment amounts would allow for different levels of activity, and the author is prepared to speak with anyone about the various options with any parties who would like to have a serious conversation. This runs counter to standard business plan presentation of, say, the original dot-com boom. The dot-com business plans created said, "Invest $X$ amount of money and the return will be $Y$." The money was invested, and a few dot-coms survived. Most dot-coms spent the money invested like drunken sailors, and the investment was lost. But what does the author know? All sorts of brilliant investment minds lost money on dot-coms, subprime bonds, Enron's, etc. The author was only the financial controller for the largest exporter out of the Bahamas while also having created from scratch both a unique macroeconomic plan

AND the multi-billion dollar business plan the reader is currently reading. Undoubtedly, this pales in comparison to the brilliance of the investment community!

The plan presented takes select existing pieces of the private Corporation X business plan and weaves them together with commentary to entertain and educate the reader. An astute reader should be able to comprehend the vision.

Three things are certain. The first is that by the time the reader reads this plan, everything Corporation X will have further evolved, for evolution is the nature of business as well as existence.

The second thing that is certain is that the author isn't sitting around waiting for the light to go on in the investment community's eyes. Other plans to self-fund Corporation X are already underway.

The third thing is that Corporation X can be used as a vehicle to take *The Byzantine Pineapple* to people on a global scale. If one understands that the macroeconomic formula presented in *The Byzantine Pineapple* can actually benefit humans globally, then one can help move the macroeconomic formula forward by helping Corporation X evolve further. Besides being a studio producing the products contained herein, the studio can be the home for organizing *The Byzantine Pineapple*'s vision. And once it gets going, it will be a profit-making home that, after paying back the initial investment, can then be used to self-fund the promotion of *The Byzantine Pineapple*'s vision.

| PRODUCT NAME | YEARS | RUN TIME MINUTES | RATING | GENRE | FILM GLOBAL BOX OFFICE REVENUE | 50% GLOBAL BOX OFFICE REVENUE | FILM PRODUCTION BUDGET | FILM MARKETING BUDGET | FILM GLOBAL ANCILLARY REVENUE | 50% GLOBAL ANCILLARY REVENUE | A+B+C+D MARKETING BUDGET | 2 YEAR GROSS PROFIT |
|---|---|---|---|---|---|---|---|---|---|---|---|---|
| TOTAL 10 YEAR PLAN | | | | | $6,550,000,000 | | | | | | | |
| PRE-PLANNING | 1-2 | | | | | | | | | | | |
| PAINLESS | 2-3 | 150 | R | DRAMEDY | | | | | | | | |
| BLINDLESS PART 1 | 3-4 | 120 | R | DRAMEDY | | | | | | | | |
| BLINDLESS PART 2 | 3-4 | 120 | R | DRAMEDY | | | | | | | | |
| TIMELESS | 4-5 | 120 | R | DRAMEDY | | | | | | | | |
| THE SALVADOR DALI CYFER | 4-5 | 120 | R | DRAMEDY | | | | | | | | |
| REMAKE #1 - "R" | 4-5 | 90 | PG-13 | FANTASY - COMEDY | | | | | | | | |
| UNMANIFEST DESTINY | 5-6 | 120 | R | DRAMA | | | | | | | | |
| H & JOB | 5-6 | 90 | PG-13 | DRAMEDY | | | | | | | | |
| REMAKE #2 - "V" | 5-6 | 90 | R | DRAMA | | | | | | | | |
| THE SALVADOR DALI CYFER #2 | 6-7 | 120 | PG-13 | DRAMEDY | | | | | | | | |
| SENATOR SMARMY | 6-7 | 120 | PG-13 | POLITICAL SATIRE | | | | | | | | |
| THE BYZANTINE PINEAPPLE | 6-7 | 90 | PG-13 | DOCUMENTARY - ESSAY | | | | | | | | |
| SUBPRIME | 7-8 | 90 | R | DRAMA | | | | | | | | |
| UNMANIFEST DESTINY #2 | 7-8 | 120 | R | DRAMEDY | | | | | | | | |
| REMAKE #3 - "I" | 7-8 | 120 | PG-13 | DRAMA | | | | | | | | |
| NLM | 8-9 | 120 | R | DRAMEDY | | | | | | | | |
| REMAKE "ROMEO AND JULIET" | 8-9 | 120 | PG-13 | SHAKESPEARE | | | | | | | | |
| THE WORST AND THE DUMBEST | 8-9 | 120 | R | DRAMEDY | | | | | | | | |
| A DAY IN THE LIFE | 9-10 | 90 | PG-13 | DRAMEDY | | | | | | | | |
| THE OLD ONES | 9-10 | 90 | R | HORROR | | | | | | | | |
| REMAKE "THE MERCHANT OF VENICE" | 9-10 | 120 | PG-13 | SHAKESPEARE | | | | | | | | |

*THE READER CAN BE ASSURED THAT THE ORIGINAL FILE CONTAINS THE FORMULA DETAILS THAT FILL IN THE BLANKS*

*IF THE READER WOULD LIKE TO KNOW MORE THE READER CAN CONTACT THE AUTHOR FOR DETAILS*

# CHAPTER 1

# Strategic Plan

THE OVERALL CORPORATION X strategic plan is very simple: create written products that target humans and then produce and market the products as books and films and merchandise.

There are two primary reasons for doing as much as possible in-house versus just creating products and selling the rights for royalties:

1. As a person without industry contacts (to start), the author knows that the offer for the rights to any product will be millionths of a penny for the products from those in the industry.
2. Those in the industry will butcher the products into something that fails if they own the rights and are left to their own devices.

Watch the brilliant Robert Altman's movie *The Player* for a cinematic presentation of the two concepts stated above. The postcard writer doesn't sell the script until he is in the position to profit greatly from the script, and Bruce Willis and Julia Roberts star in the turkey of a movie at the end.

## Plan Philosophy

Why should the author (or anyone else) believe that the products created will be purchased on a mass scale by the public is undoubtedly one question. One answer is that the author has always been one of the people in life at the end of the bell curve of normal human behavior and thought. What seems normal to the author always seems abnormal to others. However, the author has a lifetime of experience learning to effectively communicate with the masses of the bell curve and is invariably seen as a leader.

A second answer is that the author spent a decade buying and selling estates of books, comic books, magazines, and memorabilia. The author has seen more printed material than the vast majority of humans.

A third answer is that the author did take in college Shakespeare, Southern American writers, Robert Frost, E. E. Cummings, and twentieth century popular music, as well as creative writing courses. Formal literary education has been accomplished.

A fourth answer is that the author has decades of manufacturing experience. Effective creative writing (or moviemaking) is, in the author's opinion, no different than the process of manufacturing a mass-production product. The engineer creates a vision as a print, the print is tested, and then print revisions are created and tested until, through a series of iterations, a final product is arrived at.

A fifth answer is that the author matured to a point of having a purpose to creative writing. The first product designed was *UnManifest Destiny,* which has great purpose, and obviously, the author's opinion is that *The Byzantine Pineapple* has great purpose also.

There is also a market void that is perceived. This market void is detailed in an author essay titled "The Demographic Homogenization of Art (DHOA)." Now *there* is a mouthful! What DHOA posits is the following:

a. Products of art are primarily controlled for production and distribution by conglomerates.

b. Conglomerates have products produced to meet marketing demographics versus creating an actual story with a purpose.

c. Marketing demographics are defined by repetitive marketing surveys about what was popular in the past.

d. The products created are the same products as what have been made before because the purpose is to create products (books, movies, music) that are the same as what has been made before because the marketing surveys are prestructured to provide an answer that mandates creating what was created before.

e. People get bored of the same old, same old that continuously is spoon-fed to them.

f. Executives hide behind the surveys and blame the public for their failures to create products that catch hold with the public. The problem is presented as "people aren't buying the products that the people told us to make via the marketing surveys." It is the ultimate CYA.

Since the surveys always break everything down to marketing demographic, there are zero products created to attract people. This is the marketing void!

Of course, marketers will say that creating such products is "sheer fantasy." Marketers ignore the fact that, for example, men and women of all demographics continuously watch *The Godfather* and *The Matrix* movies. Well, all those marketers are industry experienced and are paid a lot of money for their jobs, so they *must* be correct. It is the people who are wrong! And when the products tank in the market, the executives blame the populace for the product failures!

That's all nice, but the products still have to be created and market-tested. Just because one has a vision and writes a book doesn't mean that crap hasn't been created. The public who doesn't know the author needs to decide.

*Painless* was written and self-published. Production of the other products already noted was started and a one-to-one market test occurred. Twenty-thousand people were met in sixteen states at 130 locations (see page 83 for the event location map). Twenty-five hundred books were sold (see page 84) for a phenomenal 12.5 percent sales rate of the author meeting people and talking to them.

To put the market test results in a different perspective:

1. The average self-published book sells one hundred copies to friends and family, and the author sold 2,500 copies across the USA to people the author doesn't know; and

2. If any manufacturing company creates a product that sells to 12.5 percent of the population across the USA without any

advertising or social media, then the manufacturing company would be considered to be sitting on a gold mine of a product.

Another way to think about this is that the vast majority of surveys performed generally are performed on about one thousand people because the sample size is then considered to be mathematically valid. A survey of twenty-thousand people is significantly more valid than the standard surveys constantly filling the news media and industry journals. The factor is greater than twenty times more valid because the validity expands exponentially.

Assume that in the USA there is a book-buying population of ten million people. If 12 percent buy without much sales work needed, then there is a low-cost no. 1 best seller waiting to happen. All the literati of the industry have to do is run the data already achieved by any mathematician/statistician for confirmation of the sales potential already documented by the first market test.

Common marketing sense states that agents or publishers would at least have an exploratory discussion about the products to see about replicating the success on a larger scale with an expanded product line. But hey, what does the lowly author know? Those industry-experienced agents and publishers are just racking up sales left and right with new authors who can sell on a mass scale. Look at what a fabulous job they are doing with product sales today!

# Event Location Map

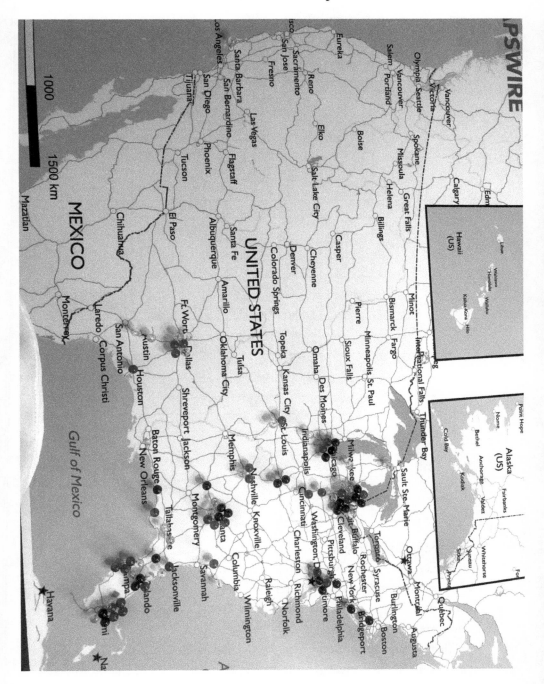

# Market Test Sales Summary Report

| Date | Location | Source | Order # | Format | Qty | Price | Col1 | Col2 | Payment |
|---|---|---|---|---|---|---|---|---|---|
| 01/15/2009 | La Vergne, Tennessee, USA | LSI Wholesale Discount | 348469 | Trade Hardback 6 × 9 | | $29.99 | 116.96 | 170.99 | Paid 4/2009 |
| | | | | | | | | | |
| **January 2009 Totals** | | | | | | | **116.96** | **17.99** | |
| | | | | | | | | | |
| 12/15/2008 | La Vergne, Tennessee, USA | LSI Wholesale Discount | 340011 | Trade Paperback 6 × 9 | 5 | $19.99 | 259.87 | 49.98 | Paid 1/2009 |
| 12/15/2008 | La Vergne, Tennessee, USA | LSI Wholesale Discount | 340011 | Trade Hardback 6 × 9 | | $29.99 | 97.47 | 15.00 | Paid 1/2009 |
| **December 2008 Totals** | | | | | **0** | | **357.34** | **64.98** | |
| | | | | | | | | | |
| 11/15/2008 | La Vergne, Tennessee, USA | LSI Wholesale Discount | 336216 | Trade Hardback 6 × 9 | | $29.99 | 155.95 | 23.99 | Paid 1/2009 |
| 11/11/2008 | Portage, Michigan, USA | Xlibris from Web | 326083 | Trade Paperback 6 × 9 | | $19.99 | 19.99 | 5.00 | Paid 1/2009 |
| **November 2008 Totals** | | | | | | | **175.94** | **28.99** | |
| | | | | | | | | | |
| 10/17/2008 | Franklin, Tennessee, USA | Xlibris from Web | 321144 | Trade Hardback 6 × 9 | | $29.99 | 29.99 | 7.50 | Paid 1/2009 |
| **October 2008 Totals** | | | | | | | **29.99** | **7.50** | |
| | | | | | | | | | |

| Total Units Sold | 2,556 |
|---|---|
| | |
| | |

In the brilliant movie *Videodrome*, the character of Max Renn asks the character of Masha why anyone would make a show of actual "snuff TV" when it is easier and safer to fake it. Masha's reply is "Because it has something that you don't have, Max. It has a philosophy. And that is what makes it dangerous."

The products created exhibit a philosophy of the *individual* in today's society. This is what gives the products power and makes the products dangerous. Contrast this to the three types of products currently pumped out by the major corporations that seemingly comprise the majority of new products:

a.  DHOA products are created to meet marketing demographics such as teens with disposable income. These products have no philosophy and therefore have "no legs."
b.  Products that espouse a right-wing philosophy that invariably comes back to "organized religion is the answer to everything" as well as "hate the left wing."
c.  Products that espouse a left-wing philosophy that invariably comes back to "good social causes solved by massive socialist government are the answer to everything" as well as "hate the right wing."

The majority of people globally are getting more and more tired of the same old, same old. People want a new vision.

The product sales vision is presented to people via an initial thirty-second book tour. All the products have such a tour. The envisioned book covers utilize the tours. The tours form the basis of the advertising construct. All that one needs to do is use one's imagination (say it like the infamous "SpongeBob, wave your hands while saying it" clip) when viewing the tours, especially when the video imagery is used for presenting the tours and one can get a real good idea of what is to be created and what the sales potential possibilities are.

Of course, an experienced production crew and marketing team can also start figuring the production and marketing costs to bring the tour to life for various formats. The business-minded author already has and is prepared to discuss all sorts of levels of production costs from self-publishing books (including foreign language and foreign distribution) through various amounts of animated video (amounts in terms of time that can be used in a variety of revenue-generating contexts) all the way through a full two-and-a-half-hour production of *Painless* as an R-rated motion picture, as well as the expected range of revenues from such ventures and how much revenue is required to breakeven.

The author has presented 130 times as well as spoke privately with many others. None met has ever seen or heard anything like the author's presentation of the thirty-second book tour.

The cover of *Painless* (see page 87) is not filled with standard marketing tripe of quoting a single adjective or two from some source. Nor does the thirty-second book tour have such hyperbole. Instead, the tours focus on the product because there is a strong enough belief in the products that the hyperbole is not needed. This also demonstrates that none of the twenty thousand people market-tested was ever actually asked to buy the *Painless* product. The book tour is presented, and the viewer is allowed to decide for themselves whether to purchase or not. The sales have been completely soft sell. The author has never asked potential customers to buy the book, and yet the author obviously sells everywhere the products are presented on a one-to-one basis.

The *Painless* thirty-second book tour, done at a leisurely one-minute pace, can be viewed at the following URL: www.poje.biz

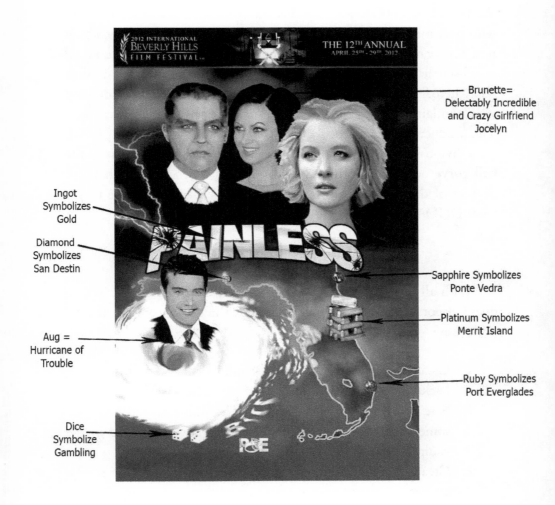

Brunette=
Delectably Incredible
and Crazy Girlfriend
Jocelyn

Ingot
Symbolizes
Gold

Diamond
Symbolizes
San Destin

Sapphire Symbolizes
Ponte Vedra

Platinum Symbolizes
Merrit Island

Aug =
Hurricane of
Trouble

Ruby Symbolizes
Port Everglades

Dice
Symbolize
Gambling

Nobody's work is universally loved. This is simple bell curve statistical math. Some will love it, and some will hate it. And then there are those who both have likes and dislikes, and they make up the meat of curve. Where the majority lies in the bell curve is the question.

From meeting twenty thousand people and having received feedback, the author can confidently state that the products failed to catch people who have a rigid mind-set about reality and, more specifically, about how a story must be constructed. For example, some people have a rigid mind-set that a story must have a very clearly and specifically defined good hero/heroine defeating a very clearly and specifically defined villain/villainess. These people do not like the products of the author. The products challenge the reality of the illusion.

Obviously, from the results of the market test, the percent of the bell curve occupied by the fixed mind-set is much smaller than the percent of the rest of the bell curve. This is expected because this is what DHOA predicts.

## Building from Here

With all of the above are established, the question now is, Where does Corporation X go from here? There are three primary tasks already underway:

1.  Create more products and publish more books, as well as picking backup on performing public events. The material presented here is only the tip of the iceberg. The author is confident that some other real doozies that no one knows about are in the vault.
2.  Create a crowdfunding event that is market test no. 2. The author is prepared to discuss what this means in terms of production and marketing costs and donations, as well as how to capture the data from the public, which proves that creating the products as motion pictures will be wildly profitable. The following marketing plan chapter expands on market test no. 2.

3.  At some point, invest in a brick-and-mortar location. Of course, such an investment means establishing a sales group and targeting customers to put newly acquired assets to work while building a studio to create portions of the movies. Everything required for production already exists, so if necessary, everything to create the film products can be contracted out. But at some point, it makes sense to establish the physical presence.

Of course, talking investment with potential investors or talking publishing with industry people or continuing to broaden the contacts interested in making Corporation X happen is always occurring. And as the succeeding sections demonstrate, the three tasks above have multiple layers involved with making them realities.

# CHAPTER 2

# Marketing Plan

T HE MARKETING SECTION has ten subsections:

A. *Further explanation of the economics of the strategic plan*

Besides the already presented ten-year plan on page 78, the following exhibits are used in the discussion:

1. Selected historical movie financial data
2. Model of *Painless* movie cost and revenues
3. Selected 2017 movie results

B. *The* Painless *movie timing schedule*
C. *An explanation of the estimated seventy-five-million-dollar production budget and twenty-five-million-dollar marketing budget*
D. *An explanation of the first market test*
E. *An explanation of the planned second market test*
F. *Overview of the second market test presentation products*
G. *Essay no. 1: A comparison of the planned* Painless *production to the recent fail of the* Ben-Hur *remake*
H. *Essay no. 2: A comparison of the planned* Painless *production to the recent fail of* The Sea of Trees
I. *Essay no. 3: A comparison of the planned* Painless *production to the production of* The Revenant
J. *Essay no. 4: The author's IMDB review of the movie* Elysium

## A. *Further explanation of the economics of the strategic plan*

Besides the already-presented ten-year plan on page 78, the following exhibits are used in the discussion:

1. *Selected historical movie financial data*

   These three pages show the revenues and production budget (obviously, production budget is not final budget) for 198 randomly selected films. Separately, the author has a spreadsheet containing the same reported numbers for each movie for the top 60 film production companies in the USA for the last twenty-five years, and the author has watched a ton of the films. So the author has a pretty good idea of what movies cost how much to make and how the revenues came in and whether or not the movies made a minimum base factor of 2.0 for global box office versus production budget.

   But of course, the author doesn't have direct moviemaking experience with making a tent-pole film. This somehow logically means that the author doesn't know what the author is talking about!

2. *Model of Painless movie cost and revenues*

   This chart shows the revenue potential of a *Painless* movie project costing $75 million to produce and $25 million to market at various global box office levels of $300, $400, $500, and $750 million, as well as $1 billion. One can compare to the selected movie revenues on the prior pages to see just what this means in terms of box office accomplishment.

   The chart also works down through hypothetical bonuses as well as return on investment factors to get down to distributable capital to all parties involved based on a hypothetical investment model. The full model is not presented here, but it is available for discussion.

Of course, the author has reviewed the model with parties who can speak to the validity of the model. Not a single one has come back and said, "This doesn't make sense." But hey, what does the author know? The author has successfully created and market-tested the products and the vision and the financial model and has been involved in managing corporations larger than a planned *Painless* movie production, but the author doesn't have direct tent-pole movie production experience. Dang it all!

3. *Selected 2017 movie results*

There are some parties that are trying to help make Corporation X's vision come to life. For example, one person wants to bring the plan to the corporate investment bankers at their employment place, but the brilliant investing minds say that without industry-experienced discussion, it is impossible. So the author took about one minute to search the internet and craft the table on page 95 to address the issue of industry experience. What this table shows is that on a dozen 2017 releases, the industry-experienced executives at the major studios managed to lose over one billion dollars on a dozen films alone. So much for industry experience! D'oh!

What's amazing is that despite decades of industry experience, executives don't realize (or care) those products that feature things such as cannibalistic baby-eating at the climax really are going to be limited for not only initial viewership but also repeat viewership. But hey, these executives have industry experience, and it is *clearly* more important than a history of results! D'oh!

| # | FILM | YEAR | RATING | RUN TIME (MIN) | RUN TIME (HR) | BOX OFFICE BUDGET | THE NUMBERS OR BOX OFFICE MOJO GLOBAL BOX OFFICE | 50% TO MOVIE THEATRES | BOX OFFICE (main sort field) | BOX OFFICE PROFIT (LOSS) | PRODUCTION TO BOX OFFICE MULTIPLE | BOX OFFICE ON BUDGET % RETURN | THE NUMBERS DOMESTIC VIDEO SALES + RENTALS | MARKETING COSTS |
|---|------|------|--------|------|------|------|------|------|------|------|------|------|------|------|
| 1 | TRANSFORMERS: DARK OF THE MOON | 2009 | PG-13 | 154 | 2:34 | $195,000,000 | $1,123,794,076 | $561,897,038 | $561,897,038 | $366,897,038 | 5.76 | 188% | $112,131,874 | |
| 2 | TRANSFORMERS: REVENGE OF THE FALLEN | 2011 | PG-13 | 149 | 2:29 | $210,000,000 | $1,123,794,076 | $561,897,038 | $561,897,038 | $351,897,038 | 5.35 | 168% | $271,057,692 | |
| 3 | TRANSFORMERS: AGE OF EXTINCTION | 2014 | PG-13 | 165 | 2:45 | $210,000,000 | $1,104,039,076 | $552,019,538 | $552,019,538 | $342,019,538 | 5.26 | 163% | $60,611,236 | |
| 4 | PIRATES 3 | 2006 | PG-13 | 151 | 2:31 | $225,000,000 | $1,060,615,817 | $530,307,906 | $530,307,906 | $305,307,906 | 4.71 | 136% | | $97,300,000 |
| 5 | THE HUNGER GAMES: CATCHING FIRE | 2013 | PG-13 | 146 | 2:26 | $130,000,000 | $864,912,963 | $432,456,482 | $432,456,482 | $302,456,482 | 6.65 | 233% | $114,559,653 | |
| 6 | THE HUNGER GAMES | 2012 | PG-13 | 142 | 2:22 | $78,000,000 | $691,247,768 | $345,623,884 | $345,623,884 | $267,623,884 | 8.86 | 343% | $216,205,522 | |
| 7 | INCEPTION | 2010 | PG-13 | 148 | 2:28 | $160,000,000 | $832,584,416 | $416,292,208 | $416,292,208 | $256,292,208 | 5.20 | 160% | $85,549,931 | |
| 8 | THE HUNGER GAMES: MOCKINGJAY PART 1 | 2014 | PG-13 | 123 | 2:03 | $125,000,000 | $752,100,229 | $376,050,115 | $376,050,115 | $251,050,115 | 6.02 | 201% | $60,448,446 | |
| 9 | FIFTY SHADES OF GREY | 2015 | R | 125 | 2:05 | $40,000,000 | $569,651,467 | $284,825,734 | $284,825,734 | $244,825,734 | 14.24 | 612% | | |
| 10 | THE MATRIX RELOADED | 2003 | R | 138 | 2:18 | $127,000,000 | $738,576,979 | $369,288,465 | $369,288,465 | $242,288,465 | 5.82 | 191% | | $50,000,000 |
| 11 | TED | 2012 | R | 106 | 1:46 | $50,000,000 | $549,368,315 | $274,684,158 | $274,684,158 | $224,684,158 | 10.99 | 449% | $130,460,186 | |
| 12 | GUARDIANS OF THE GALAXY | 2014 | PG-13 | 121 | 2:01 | $170,000,000 | $774,176,600 | $387,088,300 | $387,088,300 | $217,088,300 | 4.55 | 128% | $112,418,009 | |
| 13 | PIRATES 3 | 2003 | PG-13 | 143 | 2:23 | $125,000,000 | $658,311,224 | $329,155,612 | $329,155,612 | $204,155,612 | 5.27 | 163% | $259,700,000 | $40,000,000 |
| 14 | TRANSFORMERS | 2007 | PG-13 | 142 | 2:22 | $151,000,000 | $708,272,592 | $354,136,296 | $354,136,296 | $203,136,296 | 4.69 | 135% | $302,362,369 | |
| 15 | MALEFICENT | 2014 | PG | 97 | 1:37 | $180,000,000 | $758,410,378 | $379,205,189 | $379,205,189 | $199,205,189 | 4.21 | 111% | $73,924,627 | |
| 16 | DANCES WITH WOLVES | 1990 | PG-13 | 181 | 3:01 | $19,000,000 | $424,200,000 | $212,100,000 | $212,100,000 | $193,100,000 | 22.33 | 1016% | | $7,500,000 |
| 17 | LUCY | 2014 | R | 90 | 1:30 | $40,000,000 | $458,863,600 | $229,431,800 | $229,431,800 | $189,431,800 | 11.47 | 474% | $24,610,783 | |
| 18 | 2012 | 2009 | PG-13 | 158 | 2:38 | $200,000,000 | $766,812,167 | $383,406,084 | $383,406,084 | $183,406,084 | 3.83 | 92% | $51,898,196 | |
| 19 | PIRATES 3 | 2007 | PG-13 | 169 | 2:49 | $300,000,000 | $960,996,492 | $480,498,246 | $480,498,246 | $180,498,246 | 3.20 | 60% | | $50,000,000 |
| 20 | THE LEGO MOVIE | 2014 | PG | 100 | 1:40 | $60,000,000 | $468,760,692 | $234,380,346 | $234,380,346 | $174,380,346 | 7.81 | 291% | $109,570,658 | |
| 21 | INTERSTELLAR | 2014 | PG-13 | 169 | 2:49 | $165,000,000 | $672,720,017 | $336,360,009 | $336,360,009 | $171,360,009 | 4.08 | 104% | $27,042,314 | |
| 22 | 300 | 2007 | R | 116 | 1:55 | $60,000,000 | $456,068,181 | $228,034,091 | $228,034,091 | $168,034,091 | 7.60 | 280% | $283,230,109 | |
| 23 | THE MATRIX | 1999 | R | 136 | 2:16 | $63,000,000 | $460,279,930 | $230,139,965 | $230,139,965 | $167,139,965 | 7.31 | 265% | | $20,000,000 |
| 24 | HOW TO TRAIN YOUR DRAGON 2 | 2014 | PG | 105 | 1:45 | $145,000,000 | $618,909,935 | $309,454,968 | $309,454,968 | $164,454,968 | 4.27 | 113% | $68,646,542 | |
| 25 | BIG HERO 6 | 2014 | PG | 108 | 1:48 | $165,000,000 | $652,109,512 | $326,054,756 | $326,054,756 | $161,054,756 | 3.95 | 98% | $79,382,661 | |
| 26 | TWISTER | 1996 | PG-13 | 113 | 1:53 | $88,000,000 | $495,900,000 | $247,950,000 | $247,950,000 | $159,950,000 | 5.64 | 182% | | $20,000,000 |
| 27 | THOR: THE DARK WORLD | 2013 | PG-13 | 120 | 2:00 | $170,000,000 | $644,783,140 | $322,391,570 | $322,391,570 | $152,391,570 | 3.79 | 90% | $67,281,521 | |
| 28 | RIO | 2011 | G | 96 | 1:36 | $90,000,000 | $484,635,760 | $242,317,880 | $242,317,880 | $152,317,880 | 5.38 | 169% | $101,724,713 | |
| 29 | THE DAY AFTER TOMORROW | 2004 | PG-13 | 124 | 2:04 | $125,000,000 | $544,272,402 | $272,136,201 | $272,136,201 | $147,136,201 | 4.35 | 118% | | $43,700,000 |
| 30 | RIO 2 | 2014 | G | 101 | 1:41 | $103,000,000 | $500,188,435 | $250,094,218 | $250,094,218 | $147,094,218 | 4.86 | 143% | $51,606,175 | |
| 31 | THE FAULT IN OUR STARS | 2012 | PG-13 | 131 | 1:31 | $45,000,000 | $377,807,405 | $188,903,703 | $188,903,703 | $143,903,703 | 8.40 | 320% | $63,801,316 | |
| 32 | THE MAZE RUNNER | 2014 | PG-13 | 125 | 2:05 | $12,000,000 | $307,239,013 | $153,619,507 | $153,619,507 | $141,619,507 | 25.60 | 1180% | $40,988,206 | |
| 33 | MR. & MRS. SMITH | 2014 | PG-13 | 113 | 1:53 | $34,000,000 | $340,750,640 | $170,375,320 | $170,375,320 | $136,375,520 | 10.02 | 401% | $33,456,526 | |
| 34 | THE MUMMY | 2005 | PG-13 | 120 | 2:00 | $110,000,000 | $478,336,280 | $239,168,140 | $239,168,140 | $129,168,140 | 4.35 | 117% | | |
| 35 | THE MATRIX REVOLUTIONS | 1999 | PG-13 | 125 | 2:05 | $80,000,000 | $416,385,488 | $208,192,744 | $208,192,744 | $128,192,744 | 5.20 | 160% | | |
| 36 | WANTED | 2003 | R | 129 | 2:09 | $110,000,000 | $416,385,816 | $250,673,816 | $250,673,816 | $125,336,908 | 6.03 | 202% | | $20,000,000 |
| 37 | GONE GIRL | 2014 | R | 145 | 2:25 | $61,000,000 | $368,061,911 | $184,030,956 | $184,030,956 | $123,030,956 | 6.03 | 202% | $22,649,922 | |
| 38 | ANNABELLE | 2014 | R | 98 | 1:38 | $6,500,000 | $250,673,816 | $125,336,908 | $125,336,908 | $118,836,908 | 38.57 | 1828% | $9,082,637 | |
| 39 | THE MUMMY 2 | 2001 | PG-13 | 130 | 2:10 | $98,000,000 | $433,007,816 | $216,503,820 | $216,503,820 | $118,503,820 | 4.42 | 121% | $91,299,402 | |
| 40 | TEENAGE MUTANT NINJA TURTLES | 2014 | PG-13 | 101 | 1:41 | $125,000,000 | $485,004,754 | $242,502,377 | $242,502,377 | $117,502,377 | 3.88 | 94% | $27,581,469 | |
| 41 | NEIGHBORS | 2014 | R | 96 | 1:36 | $18,000,000 | $268,157,400 | $134,078,700 | $134,078,700 | $116,078,700 | 14.90 | 645% | $12,801,261 | |
| 42 | TAKEN 3 | 2015 | PG-13 | 109 | 1:49 | $48,000,000 | $327,656,424 | $163,828,212 | $163,828,212 | $115,828,212 | 6.83 | 241% | $25,401,880 | |
| 43 | 22 JUMP STREET | 2014 | R | 112 | 1:52 | $50,000,000 | $331,333,876 | $165,666,938 | $165,666,938 | $115,666,938 | 6.63 | 231% | $1,459,396 | |
| 44 | DUMB AND DUMBER | 1994 | PG-13 | 106 | 1:46 | $16,000,000 | $246,400,000 | $123,200,000 | $123,200,000 | $107,200,000 | 15.40 | 670% | | |
| 45 | AMERICAN PIE | 1999 | R | 95 | 1:35 | $12,000,000 | $234,723,148 | $117,361,574 | $117,361,574 | $105,361,574 | 19.56 | 878% | | $25,000,000 |
| 46 | THE MATRIX REVOLUTIONS | 2003 | R | 129 | 2:09 | $110,000,000 | $424,259,760 | $212,129,880 | $212,129,880 | $102,129,880 | 3.86 | 93% | | $29,300,000 |
| 47 | GODZILLA | 2014 | PG-13 | 123 | 2:03 | $160,000,000 | $340,934,768 | $170,467,384 | $170,467,384 | $95,467,384 | 3.18 | 127% | $71,800,225 | |
| 48 | THE IMITATION GAME | 2014 | PG-13 | 114 | 1:54 | $14,000,000 | $208,172,194 | $104,086,097 | $104,086,097 | $94,086,097 | 13.84 | 59% | $37,417,563 | |
| 49 | THE MUMMY 2 | 2009 | PG-13 | 113 | 1:53 | $15,000,000 | $207,625,144 | $103,812,572 | $103,812,572 | $88,812,572 | 9.08 | 592% | $6,429,261 | $40,000,000 |
| 50 | TAKEN | 2013 | PG-13 | 93 | 1:33 | $25,000,000 | $226,941,588 | $113,470,794 | $113,470,794 | $88,470,794 | 6.28 | 354% | $89,759,110 | |
| 51 | AMERICAN HUSTLE | 2013 | R | 138 | 2:18 | $40,000,000 | $251,171,807 | $125,585,904 | $125,585,904 | $85,585,904 | 3.00 | 214% | $17,239,356 | |
| 52 | HOW TO TRAIN YOUR DRAGON | 2010 | PG | 98 | 1:38 | $165,000,000 | $494,878,759 | $247,439,380 | $247,439,380 | $82,439,380 | 7.17 | 50% | $190,906,669 | |
| 53 | DISTRICT 9 | 2009 | R | 112 | 1:52 | $30,000,000 | $215,196,627 | $107,598,314 | $107,598,314 | $77,598,314 | 3.00 | 259% | | $25,000,000 |
| 54 | THOR | 2011 | PG-13 | 113 | 1:53 | $150,000,000 | $449,326,618 | $224,663,309 | $224,663,309 | $74,663,309 | 3.00 | 50% | $79,738,624 | $50,000,000 |
| 55 | THE HEAT | 2013 | R | 117 | 1:57 | $43,000,000 | $229,930,771 | $114,965,386 | $114,965,386 | $71,965,386 | 5.35 | 167% | $63,955,184 | |
| 56 | HORRIBLE BOSSES | 2011 | R | 100 | 1:40 | $35,000,000 | $209,638,559 | $104,819,280 | $104,819,280 | $69,819,280 | 5.99 | 199% | $34,785,041 | |
| 57 | PLANES | 2013 | PG | 92 | 1:32 | $50,000,000 | $239,258,712 | $119,629,356 | $119,629,356 | $69,629,356 | 4.79 | 139% | $78,018,905 | |
| 58 | SHUTTER ISLAND | 2010 | R | 138 | 2:18 | $80,000,000 | $296,831,073 | $148,415,537 | $148,415,537 | $68,415,537 | 3.71 | 86% | $25,458,755 | |
| 59 | GROWN UPS | 2010 | PG-13 | 102 | 1:42 | $75,000,000 | $272,223,490 | $136,111,715 | $136,111,715 | $61,111,715 | 3.63 | 81% | $60,853,595 | |
| 60 | CLOUDY WITH A CHANCE OF MEATBALLS 2 | 2013 | PG | 95 | 1:35 | $78,000,000 | $274,325,949 | $137,162,975 | $137,162,975 | $59,162,975 | 3.52 | 76% | $35,876,327 | |
| 61 | 300: RISE OF AN EMPIRE | 2014 | R | 102 | 1:42 | $110,000,000 | $337,580,051 | $168,790,026 | $168,790,026 | $58,790,026 | 3.07 | 53% | | |
| 62 | THE OTHER WOMAN | 2014 | PG-13 | 109 | 1:49 | $40,000,000 | $196,781,193 | $98,390,597 | $98,390,597 | $58,390,597 | 4.92 | 146% | $15,879,408 | |
| 63 | INTO THE WOODS | 2014 | PG | 124 | 2:04 | $50,000,000 | $212,902,372 | $106,451,186 | $106,451,186 | $56,451,186 | 4.26 | 113% | $19,411,141 | |
| 64 | NOAH | 2014 | PG-13 | 138 | 2:18 | $125,000,000 | $362,637,473 | $181,318,737 | $181,318,737 | $56,318,737 | 2.90 | 45% | $21,238,156 | |
| 65 | THE EXPENDABLES 2 | 2012 | R | 103 | 1:43 | $100,000,000 | $311,979,256 | $155,989,628 | $155,989,628 | $55,989,628 | 3.12 | 56% | $37,175,064 | $25,000,000 |

# MODELS OF REVENUE & CASH FLOW

| | $ 300,000,000 | $ 400,000,000 | $ 426,000,000 | $ 750,000,000 | $ 1,000,000,000 |
|---|---|---|---|---|---|
| GLOBAL BOX OFFICE (GBO) | | | | | |
| DISTRIBUTOR SPLIT X% | | | | | |
| GBO TO C.P.T.M        A | | | | | |
| MOVIE RENTALS (MR) (X% GBO) | | | | | |
| MOVIE SALES (MS) (X% GBO) | | | | | |
| ANCILLARY PRODUCTS (AP) (X% GBO) | | | | | |
| TOTAL MR+MS+AP | | | | | |
| DISTRIBUTOR SPLIT X% | | | | | |
| TOTAL MR+MS+AP TO C.P.T.M        B | | | | | |
| TV RIGHTS (TVR) (X% GBO)        C | | | | | |
| TOTAL C.P.T.M REVENUE        R = A+B+C | | | | | |
| X% C.P.T.M REVENUE TO CORPORATION X        E | | | | | |
| POST ROYALTY CPTM REVENUE | | | | | |
| X% INCOME TAX | | | | | |
| POST TAX CPTM REVENUE | | | | | |
| LEVEL 1 INVESTMENT + X% RETURN (2 YEAR) | | | | | |
| C.P.T.M BALANCE 1 | | | | | |
| LESS LEVEL 2 BONUS POOL | | | | | |
| C.P.T.M BALANCE 2 | | | | | |
| LEVEL 3 X% RETURN (2 YEAR) | | | | | |
| C.P.T.M BALANCE 3 | | | | | |
| C.P.T.M BALANCE 3 SPLIT | | | | | |
| X% CAST AND CREW | | | | | |
| X% SECONDARY INVESTMENT | | | | | |
| X% CORP X | | | | | |

The filled in grid has been vetted by industry experienced firms.
If the reader would like to know what the numbers look like then....contact the author!

| | production budget | Break even with no marketing | Global Box Office | Loss without marketing costs | Assuming Marketing is 50% production | total loss |
|---|---|---|---|---|---|---|
| Live By Night | $65,000,000 | $130,000,000 | $22,000,000 | ($108,000,000) | $32,500,000 | ($140,500,000) |
| Patriot's Day | $40,000,000 | $80,000,000 | $52,000,000 | ($28,000,000) | $20,000,000 | ($48,000,000) |
| A Cure For Wellness | $40,000,000 | $80,000,000 | $25,000,000 | ($55,000,000) | $20,000,000 | ($75,000,000) |
| CHIPS | $25,000,000 | $50,000,000 | $23,000,000 | ($27,000,000) | $12,500,000 | ($39,500,000) |
| Free Fire | $10,000,000 | $20,000,000 | $4,000,000 | ($16,000,000) | $5,000,000 | ($21,000,000) |
| Ghost In The Shell | $110,000,000 | $220,000,000 | $168,000,000 | ($52,000,000) | $55,000,000 | ($107,000,000) |
| King Arthur: Legend of the Sword | $175,000,000 | $350,000,000 | $148,000,000 | ($202,000,000) | $87,500,000 | ($289,500,000) |
| The Dark Tower | $60,000,000 | $120,000,000 | $118,000,000 | ($2,000,000) | $30,000,000 | ($32,000,000) |
| Mother! | $33,000,000 | $66,000,000 | $45,000,000 | ($21,000,000) | $16,500,000 | ($37,500,000) |
| Blade runner 2049 | $150,000,000 | $300,000,000 | $248,000,000 | ($52,000,000) | $75,000,000 | ($127,000,000) |
| Let The Right One in | $35,000,000 | $70,000,000 | $43,000,000 | ($27,000,000) | $17,500,000 | ($44,500,000) |
| Only The Brave | $38,000,000 | $76,000,000 | $23,000,000 | ($53,000,000) | $19,000,000 | ($72,000,000) |
| Totals | $781,000,000 | $1,562,000,000 | $919,000,000 | ($643,000,000) | $390,500,000 | ($1,033,500,000) |

# B. *The* Painless *movie timing schedule*

*Painless* is estimated to be a two-and-half-hour movie. How is this determined? The table on page 97 provides the timing estimate, which builds up to the two-and-half-hour time.

This table follows the book very closely. Segment 15 ("The First Blackout") is added, and there is an additional thirty-second "Battle of the Mermaids" that is ready to be added for the climax. Everything else can be followed along by reading the book and following the chart.

Or one can contact the author for a copy of the screenplay. While the sequencing parallels the book, the dialogue is more expanded in the screenplay. The ability to explain certain feelings via prose in a book needs rearranging for visual, and the dialogue expansion is one way to accomplish that.

Of course, the screenplay and preproduction storyboards are in many ways like the pirate's code from *The Pirates of the Caribbean* movies. It's more of a guideline as the cast and crew bring the product to life. The key is educating everyone as to what can and can't change as the two sequels are set up in the first product.

In case the concept of guidelines is questioned, the author suggests that one research the productions of the great Sergio Leone. For example, the author first looked to Sergio Leone's films for the screenplays to learn from. It turns out that the formal screenplays just simply don't exist for the Leone films (unless the author just missed out during researching). Instead, the documentation for a script that was used was more of a guideline than a 100 percent gospel script.

The author also has created three hours of prototype DVD material that can also be used to educate any interested/involved parties about the Less trilogy. The first hour covers the backstory that is brought to life through the Less trilogy. The second hour covers *Painless* as a movie. The third hour covers the sequels *Blindless* and *Timeless*. The DVDs use still images with voice-over, as well as select soundtrack songs worked in.

Speaking of the soundtrack, the timing schedule has letters *A* to *BB* noted for select film segments. These letters note twenty-eight different songs that are worked into the production. For this publication, the cross-reference list is omitted, but the author can supply the information to interested parties as necessary.

| | | | | TOTAL RUN TIME | | MINUTES | 150.74 | HOURS | 2.51 |
|---|---|---|---|---|---|---|---|---|---|

**Table 1**

| SEG # | TITLE | SEGMENT NOTES | SOUND TRACK | EST. SEG. RUN TIME (MINUTES) | CUM RUN TIME |
|---|---|---|---|---|---|
| 1 | Title | | | 0.01 | 2.01 |
| 2 | Trove Import/Export company | Sexy Icky Vicky | A | 2.00 | 2.01 |
| 3 | Where's Aunt | Sexy Icky Vicky | | 0.30 | 2.31 |
| 4 | The Dirty Customs Agent | Sexy Icky Vicky | | 0.30 | 2.61 |
| 5 | Powdering Her Nose | Sexy Icky Vicky | | 0.25 | 2.86 |
| 6 | Junk Food | Aug & Vicky | | 0.75 | 3.61 |
| 7 | Flesh | Set Up | B | 0.30 | 3.91 |
| 8 | Big Black Dick | Aug & Vicky | | 0.50 | 4.41 |
| 9 | Killer Benz | Set Up | | 0.25 | 4.66 |
| 10 | A Broken Heart | Aug's tragedy | | 1.00 | 5.66 |
| 11 | Happy Family | Set Up | | 0.25 | 5.91 |
| 12 | Stormy Sky | Robbery | C | 1.50 | 7.41 |
| 13 | Laurel Park Place Mall | double fight | D | CUM SEG 13 TIME 6.50 | 7.41 |
| 13A | We Are The Champions | Mall Fight | | 2.50 | 9.91 |
| 13B | Dinner | Aug & Mom | | 1.50 | 11.41 |
| 13C | Heist | Mall Fight | | 1.00 | 12.41 |
| 13D | Car Ride | Aug & Champions | E | 2.00 | 14.41 |
| 13E | The Knife | Aug sees Dad killed | | 1.50 | 15.91 |
| 14 | Cooked | Set Up | | 1.50 | 17.41 |
| 15 | The First Blackout | Aug & Laurie | | 0.50 | 17.91 |
| 16 | Police | Dirty cops | | 2.00 | 19.91 |
| 17 | Working Late | Set Up | | 0.01 | 19.92 |
| 18 | Dinner at Morton's | Aug & Uncle Mark | | 2.00 | 21.92 |
| 19 | The Champions | Aug & Champions | | 2.00 | 23.92 |
| 20 | Sex's | Bathroom fight | | 3.00 | 26.92 |
| 21 | Dead Men | Set Up | | 0.25 | 27.17 |
| 22 | Fat Tuesday | Set Up | | 0.25 | 27.42 |
| 23 | The Young Circle Park | A&J meetSTEAM! | F,G | 3.00 | 30.42 |
| 24 | Pros and Cons | Aug & Uncle Mark | | 2.00 | 32.42 |
| 25 | Upper Terra Mint Drive | Foreshadow | H | 0.50 | 32.92 |
| 26 | Upper Terra Mint | Aug & Joe Khan | | 2.00 | 34.92 |
| 27 | Elect Jaden Betts | Foreshadow | | 0.20 | 35.12 |
| 28 | A drive along 75th | Foreshadow | | 0.20 | 35.32 |
| 29 | Island Car Dealership | Set Up | | 0.20 | 35.52 |
| 30 | Good To Be Alive | Aug & Jocelyn | | 2.00 | 37.52 |
| 31 | Jocelyn | Jocelyn: Double Fight | I | 5.00 | 42.52 |
| 32 | Ronald Reagan | Jocelyn: Choice | J | 2.00 | 44.52 |
| 33 | Meet John Doe | Foreshadow | | 0.50 | 45.02 |
| 34 | Human Being | Freedom | K | 3.00 | 48.02 |
| 35 | Raw Power | Foreplay | L | 3.00 | 51.02 |
| 36 | Buick Makane-Big Dumb Sex | STEAM! | M | 3.00 | 54.02 |
| 37 | Marriott Arrival | Set Up | | 0.20 | 54.22 |
| 38 | Postal | Set Up | | 0.10 | 54.32 |
| 39 | | | | | |
| 40 | | | | | |

**Table 2**

| SEG # | TITLE | SEGMENT NOTES | SOUND TRACK | EST. SEG. RUN TIME (MINUTES) | CUM RUN TIME |
|---|---|---|---|---|---|
| 38 | Postal | Set Up | | 0.10 | 54.32 |
| 39 | Callipygian | Aug & Jocelyn | | 0.20 | 54.52 |
| 40 | Poolside | Aug & Jocelyn | | 0.20 | 54.72 |
| 41 | Porno | Set Up | | 0.20 | 54.92 |
| 42 | Aphrodite's | Set Up | | 0.10 | 55.02 |
| 43 | Because | Dance Scene | N | 3.00 | 58.02 |
| 44 | Suites for Two | Set Up | | 0.10 | 58.12 |
| 45 | Touch | Bedroom Steam | O | 1.00 | 59.12 |
| 46 | Suicide | Couples Fight | P | 4.00 | 63.12 |
| 47 | Stroke Me | Set Up | | 0.50 | 63.62 |
| 48 | Terminus | Detroit Chase | Q | 0.20 | 63.82 |
| 48A | The Set up | Car Steam | R | 1.00 | 64.82 |
| 48B | Chase A | Car Chase | | 4.00 | 68.82 |
| 48C | Cemetery | Interlude | | 0.75 | 69.57 |
| 48D | Tiger Stadium | Home Opener! | CUM SEG 48 TIME 10.75 | 1.00 | 70.37 |
| 48E | The River Card | Car Chase | | 4.00 | 74.37 |
| 49 | Plebs | Fight, motion gold | | 3.00 | 77.37 |
| 50 | Love Is Like Oxygen | Car Chase | S | 8.00 | 87.37 |
| 51 | Where's Mark? | Set Up | | 0.20 | 87.57 |
| 52 | Mermaids | Dream/Fantasy | | 1.00 | 88.57 |
| 53 | Cons and Pros | Aug & Uncle Mark | | 1.50 | 90.07 |
| 54 | The Lawyer | Aug & Bard Frohman | | 1.00 | 91.07 |
| 55 | San Destin | Set Up | T | 1.00 | 92.07 |
| 56 | Keith Marshall | Aug & Keith Marshall | | 1.50 | 93.57 |
| 57 | Baytowne Village | Aug & Champions | | 1.50 | 95.07 |
| 58 | Sandbestin Hilton | Set Up | | 0.10 | 95.17 |
| 59 | Burnt Pine Hole #1 | Golf Counsel/Set Up | | 2.00 | 97.17 |
| 59A | Seabiscon | Golf Counsel/Set Up | CUM GOLF TIME 8.50 | 2.00 | 99.17 |
| 61 | Pine Strewr | Golf Counsel/Set Up | | 1.00 | 100.17 |
| 62 | Pine See | Golf Counsel/Steam | | 1.50 | 101.67 |
| 63 | French Door | Golf Counsel/Set Up | | 2.00 | 103.67 |
| 64 | Greg Czmacchi | Biography/Set Up | | 1.00 | 104.67 |
| 65 | Bonefish | Set Up | | 1.00 | 105.67 |
| 66 | Angel | Aug & Angel | | 1.50 | 107.17 |
| 67 | Angel 2 | Biography/Violence | | 2.00 | 109.17 |
| 68 | French Door 2 | Angel & Jack | | 0.50 | 109.67 |
| 69 | SARS | Robbery | | 1.00 | 110.67 |
| 70 | The Prism of Diogenes | Sea Destin | X | 2.50 | 113.17 |
| 71 | Brass In Pocket | Gambling/Steam | Y | 5.00 | 118.17 |

**Table 3**

| SEG # | TITLE | SEGMENT NOTES | SOUND TRACK | EST. SEG. RUN TIME (MINUTES) | CUM RUN TIME |
|---|---|---|---|---|---|
| 72 | Opening Night | Set Up | | 1.00 | 118.17 |
| 72A | Bad Reputation | Set Up | Z | 1.00 | 118.17 |
| 72B | Jezebel | Dawn | AA | 1.00 | 120.17 |
| 72C | Stooges | Thugs | | 0.50 | 120.67 |
| 72D | Jack | Aug & Jack | | 0.50 | 121.17 |
| 72E | Dawn | Dawn | | 0.50 | 121.67 |
| 72F | Cruisin For a Bruisin | Thugs | CUM SEG 72 TIME 7.70 | 0.50 | 122.17 |
| 72G | Security | Security | | 0.10 | 122.27 |
| 72H | Keith's | Aug & Keith Marshall | | 0.20 | 122.47 |
| 72I | Attack! | Attack! | | 0.20 | 122.67 |
| 72J | Jack's House | Set Up | | 0.20 | 122.87 |
| 72K | Angel | Aug & Angel | | 2.00 | 124.87 |
| 72L | Wise Bottle | Aug & Angel | | 0.50 | 125.37 |
| 72M | Keith's 2 | Keith's 2 | | 0.50 | 125.87 |
| 73 | Boom | Jack Dough's Death | | 0.30 | 126.17 |
| 74 | Suicide | Set Up | | 0.30 | 126.47 |
| 74A | Costa Rica | Set Up | | 0.30 | 126.47 |
| 74B | Laurie | Laurie's Death | | 0.20 | 126.67 |
| 75 | Take A Dive | Kidnap | | 0.12 | 126.79 |
| 76 | Black Monday | Uncle Mark | | 0.75 | 127.54 |
| 77 | Pool | Torture | | 3.00 | 130.54 |
| 78 | Monitor | Aug & Laurie | | 0.50 | 131.04 |
| 79 | Hospital | Capture | | 0.20 | 131.24 |
| 80 | Bridge | Escape | | 0.50 | 131.74 |
| 81 | Tcga? | Interlude | | 0.25 | 131.99 |
| 82 | Climax | Hurricane Bill | | 0.30 | 132.34 |
| 82A | Gazebo | Set Up | | 0.30 | 132.34 |
| 82B | Golf | Golfing in a Hurricane | | 1.00 | 133.34 |
| 82C | Closing the Door | Hurricane Bill | | 0.60 | 133.74 |
| 82D | A Drink | Twist | | 0.75 | 134.49 |
| 82E | Golf Ball | Hurricane Bill | CUM SEG 82 TIME 16.75 | 0.25 | 134.74 |
| 82F | Little Auggie | Twist | | 1.00 | 135.74 |
| 82G | Trees | Hurricane Bill | | 0.30 | 136.04 |
| 82H | Angel | Twist | | 0.50 | 136.54 |
| 82I | The Commons | Hurricane Bill | | 0.30 | 136.84 |
| 82J | Pull the Trigger | Twist | | 0.50 | 137.34 |
| 82K | Boat | Hurricane Bill | | 0.30 | 137.64 |
| 82L | Switch | Twist | | 0.30 | 137.64 |
| 82M | Boat 2 | Twist | | 2.00 | 138.24 |
| 82N | Safand | Twist | | 0.30 | 138.34 |
| 82O | Destruction | Hurricane Bill | | 0.50 | 138.64 |
| 82P | The lantern of Diogenes | Twist | | 3.00 | 140.34 |
| 82Q | All hell breaks loose | Hurricane Bill | | 5.00 | 140.74 |
| 83 | Denouement | Escape | BB | 2.00 | 143.74 |
| 84 | Exit Credits | | | 2.00 | 150.74 |

C. *An explanation of the estimated seventy-five-million-dollar production budget and twenty-five-million-dollar marketing budget*

The *Painless* movie's projected costs and revenues are as follows:

a. $75 million to start Corporation X and to produce *Painless*
b. $25 million to market *Painless*
c. $400 million of global box office, generating $200 million net revenue to Corporation X
d. $50+ million net revenue from ancillary products (TV rights, video sales and rentals, books, etc.).

These estimates are derived from looking at productions deemed by the author to be comparable productions. As already noted, the author has looked at the budgets of all larger studio film productions for the last thirty years, so despite not having the industry experience of those who lost a billion dollars making movies released in 2017, there might be a smidgen of accuracy in revenue/cost estimation.

As head of the estimating department at a North American global tier 1 manufacturer supplying every automotive company, the author/manager/estimator had a saying, "It's an estimate, not an actual." To get actual costs requires some investment.

For example, the "car chase" scenes in *Painless* require stunt crews, and this requires negotiating with at least three stunt companies to design a final sequence of events to be shot and to get a final quote cost. It is unrealistic to expect stunt companies to take the months of planning and discussion required to get a serious final production quote unless the production company has a reason to believe the movie shoot will take place. If the stunt company, or any contract company, believes the production will occur, then they will work very hard to get the contract.

Regardless, knowing actual costs and revenue projections is not necessary to make a deal. The estimates are reasonable enough, knowing exact numbers today really does not change the conceptual plan.

The production and marketing costs and global revenue for the films below are deemed relevant (all values in millions). The sort is done by the year of production:

| Title | Year | Production | Marketing | Global Box Office |
|---|---|---|---|---|
| Blade (R) | 1998 | 45 | ? | 131 |
| The Matrix (R) | 1999 | 63 | 20 | 460 |
| The Mummy (PG-13) | 1999 | 80 | ? | 416 |
| Resident Evil(R) | 2002 | 35 | ? | 103 |
| The Matrix Reloaded (R) | 2003 | 127 | 50 | 738 |
| Pirates/Caribb 1 (PG-13) | 2003 | 125 | 40 | 658 |
| Underworld(R) | 2003 | 22 | ? | 95 |
| Mr. & Mrs. Smith (PG-13) | 2005 | 110 | 30 | 478 |
| V for Vendetta (R) | 2006 | 54 | 37 | 132 |
| Wanted (R) | 2008 | 75 | ? | 340 |
| District 9 (R) | 2009 | 30 | 25 | 215 |
| Inception (PG-13) | 2010 | 160 | ? | 832 |
| Shutter Island (R) | 2010 | 80 | ? | 296 |
| Salt (PG-13) | 2010 | 130 | ? | 295 |

Make no mistake! Creating as big a name product as any of these movies is what Corporation X is about!

## Production Cost Estimate

The 1999 production cost for *The Matrix* was $63 million (1999), *The Mummy* was $80 million (1999), *Wanted* was $75 million (2008), and *Shutter Island* was $80 million (2010). *Painless* is as complex a product as either of the four movies, but *Painless* has less CGI and less set construction.

The current *Painless* production budget also has no screenwriter or producers' fee. This immediately makes *Painless* millions less expensive compared to a normal big-budget film production.

There are five major production cost drivers to *Painless*:

1. A car chase from Cocoa to Cocoa Beach in Florida that incorporates the original select businesses and the Cape Canaveral Hospital. This is segment 48 on the timing schedule.
2. A two-stage car chase in the Detroit area. This is segment 50 on the timing schedule. The first stage is from Grosse Pointe to Belle Isle. The second stage incorporates the 1980 Detroit Tiger's home opener, requiring a digital recreation of Tiger Stadium. This chase also incorporates Joe Louis Arena, Cobo Hall, and the GM Renaissance Center. This is segment 50 on the timing schedule.
3. A very steamy car drive up I95 in Florida on a busy Friday afternoon where the scene changes from daylight to a thunderstorm with a lightning strike scattering but not crashing cars. This is segments 34 through 36 on the timing schedule. The three segments feature three different Guns N' Roses songs from *The Spaghetti Incident*—songs that actually, both lyrically and musically, tie into the characters' sexual tryst and emotion of their relationship.

   Yes, the idea/concept is to thoroughly activate the "horndogness" of the viewers. It's segment 36—the visual/audial sensation has them "ready to go"—and there are still forty-six more segments left that build on the audience.

4. A massive beach luau in San Destin at the fictional bar of Poseidon's. The luau features people and boats filling the Gulf of Mexico. This is segment 72.
5. A major hurricane finish that destroys the San Destin area as well as Poseidon's. This is segment 82.

Creating these scenes in a manner that will awe the customer not only one time but for multiple repeat viewings on video and TV is going to cost!

## Marketing Cost Estimate

There is no direct mathematical correlation between production and marketing costs and revenue. There are plenty of movies with stars and big-name directors that have bombed, so there is no correlation to name and success. The only correlation is a product that people enjoy versus a product that people do not enjoy.

The marketing budget for *The Matrix* was $20 million (1999), *Pirates of the Caribbean I* was $40 million (2003), *Mr. & Mrs. Smith* was $30 million (2005), and *District 9* was $25 million (2009). It can be argued that the $25 million estimate is a little low, but the vision is that the product sells itself. Saturation bombing of the market is not required; selective effective marketing is required. The product is designed to sell itself as much by word of mouth after release as it is by the marketing campaign.

## Revenue Estimate

Established production studios spend a lot of money continuously surveying the public to determine what projects to produce and market. The author knows this for a fact as the author receives the same surveys weekly from Global Test Market. The survey results are used to make corporate decisions about how films should be made to optimize revenue.

The survey results are undoubtedly used to project revenues. Yet more often than not, the projects that are chosen to be created do not match revenue projections and the majority of products appear to lose money based solely on box office receipts. Why should anyone believe that *Painless* will achieve a global box of $400 million when so many other products have failed to generate a box office that large?

The fourteen select films on page 99 can be classed by films that made the benchmark of $400 million at the box office and those that did not. Each film was a financial success. What separates over $400 million box office from the less than $400 million box office?

| Title | Year | Production | Marketing | Global Box Office |
|---|---|---|---|---|
| The Matrix (R) | 1999 | 63 | 20 | 460 |
| The Mummy (PG-13) | 1999 | 80 | ? | 416 |
| The Matrix Reloaded (R) | 2003 | 127 | 50 | 738 |
| Pirates/Caribb 1 (PG-13) | 2003 | 125 | 40 | 658 |
| Mr. & Mrs. Smith (PG-13) | 2005 | 110 | 30 | 478 |
| Inception (PG-13) | 2010 | 160 | ? | 832 |
| | | | | |
| Blade (R) | 1998 | 45 | ? | 131 |
| Resident Evil (R) | 2002 | 35 | ? | 103 |
| Underworld (R) | 2003 | 22 | ? | 95 |
| V for Vendetta (R) | 2006 | 54 | 37 | 132 |
| Wanted (R) | 2008 | 75 | ? | 340 |
| District 9 (R) | 2009 | 30 | 25 | 215 |
| Shutter Island (R) | 2010 | 80 | ? | 296 |
| Salt (PG-13) | 2010 | 130 | ? | 295 |

The answer is the level of how strong the primary plot is with respect to the plot being a love story first versus being a genre story first. To achieve a global box office of $400 million, the film must draw both men and women. The story must be entertaining, but the primary story is a love story disguised as a different style of story:

1. The Matrix trilogy is a love story of Neo and Trinity disguised as a science-fiction story.
2. *The Mummy* is a love story of Rick and Evie disguised as a horror story.
3. The *Pirates* trilogy is a love story of William Turner and Elizabeth Swann disguised as an adventure story.
4. *Mr. & Mrs. Smith* is a love story of Pitt/Jolie's title characters disguised as an action story.
5. *Inception* is a love story of Dom and Mal disguised as a science-fiction story.
6. *Blade* is first and foremost a vampire story with the female lead not really a love interest for Blade.
7. *Resident Evil* is first and foremost a zombie story with the love interest only revealed at the end.
8. *Underworld* is a vampire/werewolf story that makes the love interest secondary.
9. *V for Vendetta* is not a couple's love. The male/female leads share a love but not as a couple.
10. *Wanted* never develops a love story; it is an action story.
11. *District 9* never develops a love story; it is a reality show / science-fiction story.
12. *Shutter Island* never really develops the love story; it is an action story.
13. *Salt* never develops a love story; it is an action story.

*Painless* (the Less trilogy) is the love story of Aug and Jocelyn. The story is also a love triangle involving Aug's dead wife, Laurie, who died when Jocelyn was sent to murder her. Aug and Jocelyn love each other, but how can they trust each other? *Painless* accomplishes the love story thematic that appeals to women while providing action and sexy characters that both men and women enjoy. Where women go, men follow.

In 1999, both *The Mummy* and *The Matrix* each had a global box office of $400+ million. The marketing thematic between *Painless* and *Mummy/Matrix* is very similar. These are all love stories disguised as different types of stories (*The Mummy* as horror, *The Matrix* as science fiction, *Painless* as crime*)* with fate and destiny driving the characters with specifically constructed, very physical action-and-chase scenes. (*Painless* takes the physical romance a bit further hence the adult rating.) There's also been thirteen years of ticket price increases.

It must also be noted that *The Matrix Reloaded* (2003) generated $738 million and *Inception* (2010) generated $832 million of global box office. If *Painless* is able to generate global box office revenue anywhere near those numbers, then Corporation X has sequels *Blindless* and *Timeless* ready to go. Corporation X will be a cash cow.

The *Painless* construction and marketing videos (DVD1) go through the product design and test-marketing done to prove the marketability of *Painless* (the Less trilogy) and the other Poje, LLC products. These videos explain why *Painless* will be more successful than, say, *Blade* or *District 9*. Suffice to say here that *Painless* is specifically designed to appeal to adult men and women around the globe.

With respect to the other revenue projections, the following projections are taken from reviewing the numbers on the select film cost revenues on page 93. These projections are intended to be considered conservative.

| | |
|---|---|
| TV rights: | For the few documented films, the rights sales of *Conan 3-D*, *V for Vendetta*, and *Underworld* are all in the $25 million range, so the value of $25 million is used. |
| Video rentals: | *The Mummy* and *Pirates* movies generated sales of $75+ million of video rentals of which 50 percent flows to the production company. A value of $25 million is used for video rentals. |
| Video sales: | *The Mummy* generated sales of $63+ million of video sales of which 50 percent flows to the production company. A value of $25 million is used for video sales. |

Ancillary products:    Ancillary products are books, clothes, video games, etc. If *Painless* generates $400 million of global box office, then all sorts of merchandising are selling. A value of $10 million net revenue to Corporation X is used for ancillary products.

But hey! What does the nonindustry-experienced author know? The nonindustry-experienced author just presented the reader with a more rational explanation about movie revenues than the industry-experienced people who lost $1+ billion on movie products in 2017 probably could ever do. But they have industry experience! D'oh!

Ask yourself this question: Who do you really think understands what people want from art products better, the nonindustry-experienced author or those industry-experienced people who lost $1+ billion in 2017?

## D. *An explanation of the first market test*

The author, being an experienced businessperson, knew before starting the product design process that the experienced book and movie people would not take to what the author was creating. This just naturally follows the fact that the author is creating products to address a market void that the experienced book and movie people don't recognize as even existing!

This being true, the author knew that the only way to succeed is to get in front of people and sell product one to one, while at the same time, never hard selling to any potential customer directly. The question was, How to accomplish this?

The first market test started with the product and book cover design. The construction of the story and the book cover facilitated the thirty-second book tour.

The first public event was at the Border's Bookstore (RIP) in Jensen Beach, Florida. There was only the first book, and the display erected only showed one book as work was just beginning on both the sequel and other products. The book tour was quite stumbling to start as it hadn't been repeated enough times to hone the speech. Despite all the prior, the author outsold all the other self-published authors the store had ever hosted. The author was given carte blanche to not only return to the Jensen Beach store but word also went out to other store managers to allow the author to come in and display.

The routine was to show up for the opening at 10:00 AM and to stay until 6:00 PM. As long as the next customer through the door was over eighteen, the author would greet the customer and then ask if the author could give the customer a bookmark. If the customer said yes, the author would inform the customer that the bookmark was for the author's first book—a crime novel. The author would then ask, "Do you like crime novels?" If the answer was yes, then the author would ask, "May I give you a thirty-second book tour?" More often than not, the customer would say yes, and most were laughing heartily by the time the tour was completed.

From there, the spiel professionalized, the product line grew, the displays grew, the *Painless* screenplay was written, and twenty thousand people were personally met at 130 events in sixteen states. This included a three-day stint at BookExpo America over one year as well as the screenplay getting attendance at the Beverly Hills Film Festival. Everywhere the Poje-show traveled, the people were blown away by the unique products. The vast majority of the people met had fun, and product was sold everywhere.

In case the twenty-thousand-people count is questioned, not only did the author hand out more bookmarks than that but also the math works out as follows:

> Twenty thousand divided by 130 events is equal to an average of 154 people per day (assuming a single day for each event). For an eight-hour day, that works out to about 20 people per hour or a new person on average every three minutes. If the reader thinks this is impossible, then the reader is stating that less than 20,000 people were met. This means that the sales rate achieved is even *greater* than the 12.5 percent of people met who took the book tour!

Obviously, the one-to-one marketing is successful, and the author can continue to publish and grow sales just by meeting the public and presenting products anywhere any day. The next step is to translate the one-to-one marketing to a one-to-many marketing.

## E. *An explanation of the planned second market test*

Translating the successful one-to-one market test to a controlled one-to-many market test is conceptually very easy. Create a crowdfunding event based on the one-to-one model, and let the public decide the product viability. Assuming the same success rate of 12.5 percent or a lower rate of, say, 5 percent or whatever rate one chooses to decide on that is reasonable, then one can compare the targeted results for a minimum twenty-five-dollar donation for the public expected to reach to see if costs are projected to be covered.

The real purpose of the test is not to raise capital, although the expectation is that that will most definitely occur as a by-product of the event. The real purpose of the event is to harvest email addresses of donors. The crop is expected to be such a bumper crop that the financial and entertainment industries simply cannot ignore the results. Someone's greed will overtake any dislike of the products.

Besides the obligatory web page text, the primary focus of the crowdfunding event would be the video. The vision is to have an animated five-minute presentation of ten products followed by a one-to-two-minute speech by the author. The planned giveaway for the twenty-five-dollar donation is a copy of *The Byzantine Pineapple* without the Corporation X business plan. Larger donations can receive a different giveaway set of products.

Most authors/filmmakers on crowdfunding sites seemingly showcase a single product, and most of the time, they don't really focus on the product. They focus on who will be acting or directing or about some form of hyperbole that some media has attached to the product. The planned five-minute animation has none of that. The construct is all about the products:

| | |
|---|---|
| Introduction | 12 seconds |
| *Painless* | 45 seconds |
| *Blindless* | 30 seconds |
| *Timeless* | 30 seconds |
| *UnManifest Destiny* | 45 seconds |
| *The Salvador Dali Cyfer* | 45 seconds |
| *H & Job* | 20 seconds |
| *Senator Smarmy* | 20 seconds |
| *Subprime* | 20 seconds |
| *NLM* | 20 seconds |
| *The Byzantine Pineapple* | 15 seconds |

That's 302 seconds, or just over five minutes, for an intro plus ten products. No one anywhere else on planet earth has either such a vision or the products capable of making such a vision work.

The author, as a businessperson, has lined up an animation studio to create the 2-D and 3-D imagery. The animation company does work on advertising animation for an NBA team and the major cruise lines, as well as other corporations. The owner of the animation company will very likely get one of the first signed copies of *UnManifest Destiny*. The owner gets the complete vision.

| | INTRODUCTION — 15 SECONDS |
|---|---|
| TITLE | INTRODUCTION |
| MUSIC | ROCK ROCK TIL YOU DROP / DEF LEPPARD (INTRO) |
| MAJOR FEATURES | CORPORATION X LOGO (CENTERED) / OTHER PRODUCT NAMES SWIRL AROUND THE LOGO |

| | TIMELESS — 30 SECONDS |
|---|---|
| TITLE | TIMELESS |
| MUSIC | COMES LOVE / ARTIE SHAW |
| CHARACTERS | AUG |
| LOCATIONS | WEEKI WACHEE, WILDWOOD, NJ; SAINT ARMANDS, FL; TIMES SQUARE |
| MAJOR FEATURES | MERMAIDS; SAINT ARMANDS; SEX IN CADILLAC; ELECTRICAL STORM; V-J DAY 1 UNCONDITIONAL SURRENDER |

| | E. & J.R. — 30 SECONDS |
|---|---|
| TITLE | E. & J.R. |
| MUSIC | NONE |
| CHARACTERS | VILLAGE IDIOT; PRESIDENT FOOLIO; MIKE GRAFTON |
| LOCATIONS | FACTORY |
| MAJOR FEATURES | TERMINATED EMPLOYEE; SUICIDE / TRUE STORY WITH ACTUAL OBITUARY |

| | JLN — 30 SECONDS |
|---|---|
| TITLE | JLN |
| MUSIC | PETER TOSH |
| CHARACTERS | JUMBO KLAAT; KIDDIELAND ROO; ANITA, MOUND; EHGH-X; AD CHARACTERS |
| LOCATIONS | DETROIT; ATLANTA; ORLANDO; CINCINNATI |
| MAJOR FEATURES | FOX THEATRE; CHASE SCENES; EXPLOSIONS / "BE AN OCTOMOM TODAY" AD |

| | ORTIZ — 15 SECONDS |
|---|---|
| TITLE | ORTIZ |
| MUSIC | FRANK SINATRA |
| MAJOR FEATURES | CORPORATION X LOGO (CENTERED) / Animation with ram butting dam using Corporation X logo |

| | PABLOS — 45 SECONDS |
|---|---|
| TITLE | PABLOS |
| MUSIC | LOVE IS LIKE OXYGEN / BAD REPUTATION / SWEET / REVEREND HORTON HEAT |
| CHARACTERS | AUG & JOCELYN (4 versions of J) |
| LOCATIONS | FORT LAUDERDALE; MERRITT ISLAND; PONTE VEDRA; SAN DESTIN; DETROIT; PHILADELPHIA; CLEVELAND |
| MAJOR FEATURES | HURRICANE; JEWELS; JAGUAR; GAMBLING; MERMAID; GOLF / THE RING OF LOVE; 2 CAR CHASES |

| | THREE KNOT PARTY? — 45 SECONDS |
|---|---|
| TITLE | THREE KNOT PARTY? |
| MUSIC | JOAQUIN RODRIGO / CONCIERTO HEROICO |
| CHARACTERS | ANFIO FLORES & FAMILY; SOCIALIST PROFESSOR; GENERAL; CHANDRA LEVY INTERN |
| LOCATIONS | HONDURAS; UNITED NATIONS; WASHINGTON DC |
| MAJOR FEATURES | EXPLOSIONS; EARTHQUAKE; MASS RIOTING IN MULTIPLE CITIES / PRESS CORP |

| | BEATON HEART? — 30 SECONDS |
|---|---|
| TITLE | BEATON HEART? |
| MUSIC | MATERIAL GIRL / MADONNA |
| CHARACTERS | SENATOR SHANK; PRESIDENT NAPOLEON |
| LOCATIONS | MANOR; ANIMAL FARM |
| MAJOR FEATURES | METAPHORIC IMAGERY COMPARING ORWELL'S ANIMAL FARM / TO THE CAST OF CHARACTERS |

| | THE STAR SPANGLED BANNER — 15 SECONDS |
|---|---|
| TITLE | THE STAR SPANGLED BANNER |
| MUSIC | NONE |
| CHARACTERS | |
| LOCATIONS | WASHINGTON DC |
| MAJOR FEATURES | FEATURES OF A UNIQUE FLAT TAX FORMULA AND RESTRUCTURING OF GOVERNMENT |

| | HAIR GLOB? — 30 SECONDS |
|---|---|
| TITLE | HAIR GLOB? |
| MUSIC | BIG DUMB SEX / SOUNDGARDEN |
| CHARACTERS | AUG & ICKY VICKY |
| LOCATIONS | SAN DESTIN; MIAMI; MICHIGAN; DETROIT; CHICAGO; PHILADELPHIA |
| MAJOR FEATURES | EXPLODING DEER BLIND; DISCO DEMOTION NIGHT; SHOWGIRLS / 2 CHASES; ICE STORM; KING OF PRUSSIA MALL |

| | THE BALLROOM DALL CITIES — 45 SECONDS |
|---|---|
| TITLE | THE BALLROOM DALL CITIES |
| MUSIC | BEDTIME STORIES / MADONNA |
| CHARACTERS | FLATEI, FIPERLETTE, PFERLAI, BLJACHEN KONG, LEONARDO; DEMON DODGOZL |
| LOCATIONS | TAMPA, WASHINGTON DC; SHANGHAI; THE ALPS, SPAIN |
| MAJOR FEATURES | BOOK OF SURREALISM; WORKS OF DALI; NATIONAL GALLERY IN DC / MAGIC |

| | SURPRISE — 30 SECONDS |
|---|---|
| TITLE | SURPRISE |
| MUSIC | RITUAL DRUM DANCE / TITO PUENTE |
| CHARACTERS | DANIELLA; DAUGHTER; SON; EX: LOVER: PRIEST |
| LOCATIONS | MIAMI AREA |
| MAJOR FEATURES | JESU CHURCH IN MIAMI; QUINCEANERA / CHASES; VIOLENCE |

| | POME TIME? — 6 MINUTES |
|---|---|
| TITLE | POME TIME? |

**Read Across**

The cost of creating the animation depends on what the overall plan is. The five-minute video can be created, or more than five minutes can be created. If more animation is created, then longer materials can be placed on YouTube or other internet locations or in select advertising.

It so happens that the animation company is also prepared for translation into Spanish, Portuguese, and French. The animation could be translated into these languages, which opens the possibility of expanding the crowdfunding to other countries. If the published books are translated and published in foreign countries, the distribution cost of the products is minimized. Of course, this means issues with respect to information systems and data gathering, as well as issues regarding banking and legal permissions. Of course, such a plan then adds cost and time, but the payoff is the proof of global support for the products.

Speaking of legal, a Beverly Hills entertainment industry law firm located on Wilshire Boulevard, is lined up to handle all the legal permissions for things such as, say, any music used in the animation video. The law firm is also prepared for things such as the approximate one hundred hours of preproduction legal work needed for producing *Painless* as a big-budget motion picture and all the other legal issues entailed.

The author's presentation would require a preliminary shoot and a final shoot. A set of the author's products need creating. The plan is that the two minutes is a continuous shot with motion so the preliminary can work out the bugs. At the end of the shoot, the author would ask for support via the supplying of an email address to get on a quarterly Corporation X newsletter (plus giveaway), which tacitly means a minimum twenty-five-dollar donation, as well as being prepared to deliver on the quarterly newsletter.

The whole process is created to be portable. This way, the presentation can be established on not just a single crowdfunding site but also on multiple crowdfunding sites simultaneously.

The event is quite information systems heavy. Corporation X has to be prepared to do the following:

1.  Gather marketing data from the crowdfunding site(s) about how many views of the site occur.
2.  Prepare the database to harvest the data from every placement if the expanded placement on other sites or select advertising is done (*data* means data about viewing frequency and other marketing data).
3.  Gather the donor information from the crowdfunding site(s) into the Corporation X database.
4.  Generate all the mailing labels necessary or export the mailing label data necessary for a contract company to mail out giveaways.
5.  Have the ERP/accounting system ready for data processing of all the receipt/distribution data.
6.  Have a revamped website (like poje.biz) for customers to browse as well as to reflect Corporation X.
7.  Be prepared to rapidly translate the marketing data for use in raising the capital required to create *Painless*—the movie.

This gets real hairy if foreign languages are involved, but the author, as a businessperson, has already designed and installed information systems larger and more complex than anything involved here. The information system should not be an issue.

## F. *Overview of the second market test presentation products*

So what are the video products? These are all completely original products wherein sequencing has been determined for the most part by the responses to the first market test. The imagery is not included, but the imagery can be provided to match up with the book tours.

The lead product obviously is the Less trilogy (*Painless, Blindless,* and *Timeless*). The text for the tours are as follows:

## Painless

It's 2005. The man with the hurricane full of trouble is Augustus Valentine. Aug runs an import/export company in Port Everglades that was started with illegal money; so were the real estate developments in San Destin. People with illegal money must do something with it. Periodically, goods are smuggled in and out of the country; in comes the rubies, sapphires, and diamonds. They are promptly stolen from Mr. Aug. Who did what and why is the primary plot.

*Painless* also features Jocelyn—Aug's crazy girlfriend. Jocelyn sells Jaguars in Merritt Island. They have a weekend getaway in Ponte Vedra. There's a big hurricane finish on the beach in San Destin with gold, platinum, and gambling in the mix, as well as character development chapters in Detroit, Philadelphia, Cleveland, and Nashville.

## Blindless

*Blindless* features the following:

- The back end of the hurricane
- Deer hunting, car chases, and fireworks in Saranac
- Kruggerands in Detroit and Disco Demolition Night in Chicago
- Extended chase scenes through South Florida (South Beach in particular)
- An extended chase scene through the Lincoln Road Mall
- *Blindless* winds up with an ice storm in Philadelphia, followed by a car chase down the Schuylkill (the Sure-Kill) Expressway to Penn's Landing and also an extended chase scene through the King of Prussia Mall

## Timeless

*Timeless* concludes the Less trilogy with the following:

- Some "wild wood" in Wildwood

- Mermaids in Weeki Wachee
- Chases through the biotechnology corridor of New Jersey
- Cars crashing in Saint Armand's and Unconditional Surrender in Sarasota
- A car chase through Cleveland and
- Winds up with a Halloween electrical storm in New York City with fights in Zuccotti Park and Wall Street
- Climax with a chase and fight in Times Square and with more Unconditional Surrender

The King of Prussia Mall—the "cat's pyjamas" mall of the northeast—has already indicated their support and willingness for *Blindless* as demonstrated by the excerpt of an email dialogue between the author and mall representatives:

> I'm pleased to notify you that the King of Prussia Mall has approved your request for the use of its floor plans, as provided in PDFs on the website, in your upcoming book *Blindless*. Best of luck in completing the book, and we wish you great success in the book sales and ambitions for a feature film production.

Obviously, the King of Prussia Mall buys off on *Blindless*.

Ask yourself these questions:

How many companies, like the King of Prussia Mall (the largest retail space mall in America), will want to have product placement inside the Less trilogy?

**The answer is that many companies will!**

How many people will repetitively pay to watch an extended dramatic and humorous chase through the King of Prussia Mall?

**The answer is that millions of people will!**

# UnManifest Destiny

Capitalism teaches that entities must grow or die. The same construct is true for countries. How is the United States growing? What will be the fifty-first state? This is the "unmanifest destiny" of the United States.

Honduras is under attack from leftist rebels funded by the Chavezistas. They have negotiated footholds in Nicaragua and El Salvador from which to attack from. Oil money is funding the insurrection and so is drug money. The Mexican Zeta drug cartels have a hand in the game.

The president of Honduras is assassinated. A power vacuum exists that needs to be filled. A series of political candidates suddenly appear, seeking the presidency. One candidate is Consuela DeLa Varague—the Socialist University professor. Another candidate is Wilfredo De Rota—a Honduran army general.

Another candidate is Antonio Flores—a charismatic Honduran family man. Antonio emerges as a front-runner campaigning on a unique platform—having Honduras become the fifty-first state of the United States. The rebel and drug cartels would then be put down by the US military, who would now be protecting the borders of the fifty-first state of the USA. Also, the citizens of Honduras would be beneficiaries of massive financial aid programs, and all illegal immigration of Hondurans to the US would magically disappear.

The Chavezistas and drug cartels are mortified of this possibility and so are the Chinese, the United Nations, and neighboring countries in Latin America, as well as a contingent of politicians in America. They go all in with the competing candidates. They decry the so-called ugly American, and cash flows into their coffers from all over.

Also, flowing into Honduras is the international press corps. They all are digging for dirt on Antonio Flores. Whose back pocket is he in?

Antonio has his own personal issues with attacks on both his family and his life. Rumors exist of an affair between Antonio and an attractive young American consulate worker. The female has disappeared, and allegations are being leveled. Can Antonio trust his friends and political allies?

An earthquake rips apart San Pedro Sula. Foreign aid, both wanted and unwanted, flows into the country. In Honduras, the US, Latin America, South America, and Europe are protests for and against the aid and also the concept of a Central American country becoming a new US state. Puerto Rico erupts over the concept of the fifty-first state being a Latin American country. The reverse domino effect is feared that the United States Constitution will grow like a college super conference.

Allegations are made that the earthquake was created by the US as an excuse to get US troops into Honduras. Is this real?

Among the earthquake wreckage, the dismembered body of the missing American girl is discovered in a freshly unearthed tomb. How did her body get there? Americans are urged to protest the outrage of her murder.

The first story climaxes with a massive political rally in Tegucigalpa, which literally explodes. Who caused the explosions? Do Tony and his family survive unscathed? And how do the Honduran people vote, and who is performing the count of the votes?

## The Salvador Dali Cyfer!

Once upon a time in Tampa lived the Ample-Alliswell sisters! The sisters were magical witches, only they never knew it.

The oldest sister is Pleud. She could move things with her mind. The middle sister is Piperswife. She had some tricks up her sleeve. The youngest sister was Pfeelmi. She is an empath.

Together, they are *the Ample Ones!*

The Ample Ones travel to the Salvador Dali Museum in Tampa. They find themselves trapped in a mysterious, hidden chamber in the museum where they find and read from the Mysterious Book of Surrealism.

A demon appears and attacks the Ample Ones. Their powers come to life and protect them. They read from the Book of Surrealism and learn how to "Cube" themselves through space and time. The Ample Ones Cube to the hall where they find themselves at the painting of *Geopoliticus Child*.

A dead body is on the floor, and sirens are heard. The sisters look at the painting where a mysterious message appeared:

### *Pleud Bong* _____ _____

The sisters realize they are trapped in a global conspiracy—a conspiracy that can only be overcome by solving the Salvador Dali Cyfer!

Soon, the Ample Ones are fleeing other demons and Cubing to Balerna, Switzerland, to find the secrets locked inside the *Space Venus* sculpture, to Paris and Shanghai to find the secrets of the *Persistence of Memory* and the *Surrealist Piano*, to Courchevel, France, for the *Space Elephant* enigma, as well as chasing through the Dali Theatre Museum in Figueres, Spain.

Along the way, they meet guys such as Leonardo, the artist, and Interpol Detective Blacchus Kohl. Demons such as the nefarious Dodil are also encountered.

The climax of the first story is in the National Gallery of Art in Washington, DC, wherein the answer to the riddle of global conspiracy known as the Salvador Dali Cyfer lies hidden inside Dali's the *Sacrament of the Last Supper*.

## H & Job

Politicians and businesspeople talk about jobs all the time. The fact is that the picture painted about jobs is all phony. They never talk about the BS that goes on that comes with having a job.

The Village Idiot is in charge of product estimating at Corporation H. Over a six-year period, the Village Idiot helped turn around the financial fortunes of a twenty-year-old subsidiary of a global Japanese manufacturing concern by the product estimating work performed by the Village Idiot. The supportive president is Juro Nakayama, and three employees report to the Village Idiot: the Ginker-Loba of the Universe (GLOTU), the Suck-Pig of the Universe (SPOTU), and Dean the Doggie Killer.

Suddenly, President Juro suffers a debilitating stroke, and Japan hires in Foolio from outside the company to be the new president. This opens the door for the manufacturing manager, Dr. Evil, to make a play to gain control of product estimating.

One Friday, the Village Idiot is summoned to Foolio's office and told to fire SPOTU. The reason given is to reduce the growing overhead of the corporation.

The Village Idiot points out that SPOTU's job is administrative. There will be a zero reduction in overhead. So just what is the reason for being told to fire SPOTU? The answer given is that "this is the first of more to come, and the Village Idiot must lead the way."

The Village Idiot replies that the task will be done, but that he will no longer work nights, lunches, or weekends. The Village Idiot tells SPOTU, an ex-navy and seven-year-plus employee who had worked his way off the factory floor to an office job, the news.

SPOTU plays softball on the coed team that night and is asked why he is terminated. SPOTU is asked by Heather, the low person on the pole in manufacturing engineering and single mother to a three-year-old, why he is fired. SPOTU tells her what he is told: "He is the first of more to come."

Heather is a basket case at work next Monday. Her boss asks why. Heather says that she doesn't know how she is going to take care of her daughter when she is fired. Her boss goes and asks Foolio whether Heather will be fired on Friday.

Foolio's response is to send SPOTU a letter threatening SPOTU's meager severance. SPOTU's response is to take a shotgun to his head and blow it off.

**Michael Earl Grafton (1971–2003)**

## Senator Smarmy

Senator Smarmy is a combination of short stories as well as a full-length musical. The general concept is that politicians globally seem to repetitively act in one of two manners. The first manner is sheer arrogance, hence the name Smarmy. The second manner is that they view themselves personally as a voluptuous or well-hung porn star who gets paid for services, hence the name Smilfme.

The storyboard on page 120 is the prototype presentation of the Senator Smarmy musical *Party Late* (themed after the Party Gate event). Repetitive story characters Aarrgghh and Hip Pop Crissy crash the party as the Saliciouslys (instead of the Salahis). The party is at the wind-powered Manor Farm (where *Animal Farm* takes place).

The musical has three segments. The first segment is Aarrgghh and Hip Pop crashing the party. During this segment, they are transformed into Party members at the dinner (*Gooble-Gobble one of us*). The second segment features the transformed Aarrgghh and Hip Pop playing games, such as Washingtoga Squares, for money and prizes as rewards for their transformation (see page 122). The last segment features Aarrgghh and Hip Pop waking up from their transformation.

The musical is envisioned as a framework where certain sections can be changed out as current political events crop up. The political parties and their acolytes continuously provide fodder.

The musical has evolved from the earlier mock-up with the opening number now being the song "American Sham" (complete with patriotically and skimpily dressed dancers). The following is an excerpt of the opening:

On the trail for two hundred days
Last night a little rock
Act like Jenna Haze

Sweet, sweet Smilfme
Come catch her act
She'll do the big PACS
With her unnatural facts

On top of
Her donor's thing
Can't you hear her
"Poke Me" she does sing!

For your vote
She will fight
You're gonna see her make it
In the show tonight

She's an American sham
She's an American sham
She's gone to Washington
She's going to Party down
She's an American sham

# Senator Smiffne Smarmy presents:

## PARTY LATE!

### THE MUSICAL!

**PRESIDENT "ALL ANIMALS ARE CREATED EQUAL" NAPOLEON HOSTS A HALLOWEEN PARTY AT MANOR FARM!**

Arngh and Hip Pop crash the party! They don't come dressed as the *Stalin's* 2!

Chairman Hou is at the Party...He is dressed as a Capitalist!

Fred Reserve is at the Party... He is dressed as a Communist!

Senatorial Candidate Iyama Bee Itch attends. She is a Witch!

Senator Smarmy comes as :: first, *She Wolf of The US*

**Also Attending:**

| | |
|---|---|
| SIR RAMADEER!!! | PHEASANTS!!! |
| CONSPIRACY BROTHER!!! | WHITE WATER ARKANSAS!!! |
| THE ORWELLS!!! | SENATOR MARILYN & MORE!!! |

Smiffme Here!

**Coming for you!**

Senator Smarmy in The DikkiLeaks Scandal (Part 1)

Smiffme vs. Sy1ghme
In
The Story of "Oh! Bootsmutts"

# A VERY P.C. Musical!

WASHINGTOGA SQUARES

The Orwells perform:   **Back In the US a China**
**Viva! Bought Congress**

Napoleon gets the party started:   **Big Nappy!**

Napoleon Jokes and Preaches before singing:
**The Lord Has Mercy for their Votes**

Brown Fox performs exorcism with:   **Let's Move...On.Org**

TortoiseElvis & Dreadful Zeppelin sing   **The Immigration Song**

Iyama Bee Itch & Sir Ramadeer star in   **"I am Not a Witch"**

Sir Ramadeer sings:   **Witch Wired Up**

The Gibbons Monkey polls a game of BINGO!

**B     I     N     G     O**
BODES   IMPOVERISHED   NAPOLEON   GOVERNMENT   OMG!
SANENGAD

The Orwells come back on stage:   **TarpNo?**
**None of US got Nothin' to Hide**
**Senior Smarmy**

Senator Marilyn sings:   **Sweet Painted Smiffme!**

Senator Smarmy sings:   **Freddie Mac Farm**

Smiffme rolls on stage:   **We're All Virgins**

Senator Smarmy Opens Wallets:   **Material Pol**

Conspiracy Brother Raps!   **The Revolution Is Transparent**

& Sings!   **Riot!**

Napoleon Encores:   **Generation Avalanche**
**High Speed Rail**
**Napoleon**

Also Featuring the parallel stories of

| Dieter Rhhostrich | Bot Pusebores |
|---|---|
| The Struggle | The Book |
| Boom & Bust Part 1 | Boom & Bust Part 2 |
| Mochtkraveltkmp | Mochtliibermohne |
| The Father | The Prophet |
| September | September |
| The Mentor 2 | The Mentor 2 |
| The Jewish Problem 1 | The Jewish Problem 2 |

# WASHINGTOGA SQUARES

YOUR HOST
WILLIAM RILEY

PLAYING FOR THE BIG O
AUDREY
"PACMAN"
JONES III

PLAYING FOR X + $
WALLACE STREET

REP. TRANSPARENCY | CHAIRMAN MAO | FRED RESERVE

SENATOR MARILYN | SENATOR SMARMY | SENATOR TAUPE

HIP HOP CRISSY | ARRGH UMENT | GOVERNESS SURELOVEM PALING

THE YOGURT AMAZONS =

MARGIE O. WRECK     GRETL HARLOTSON

# Subprime

Daniella is a Miami area real estate agent. It is 2007, and Daniella is trying to close her largest subprime deal ever for some estates in Coral Gables. It's just the biggest version yet of the same deals Daniella has been pushing ever since she came to America fifteen years prior.

Daniella has issues to deal with. Like the loans she arranges, Daniella is subprime to

1. her bitter ex-husband,
2. her gigolo,
3. her daughter and the Quinceañera being arranged,
4. her disapproving son,
5. her disapproving Catholic church,
6. the bankers making the deal and squeezing her for kickbacks,
7. her boss arranging the deal and squeezing her for more than kickbacks,
8. the INS agents squeezing her for everything they can get, and
9. the Haitians who are her original customers but now violently after her because the balloon payment came due.

Like the loans she arranges, Daniella is "subprime."

# The Byzantine Pineapple

*The Byzantine Pineapple* is published separately. *The Byzantine Pineapple* is a nonfiction essay that proposes a completely new macroeconomic formula for budgeting governments, as well as reform of *socioeconomic legal political systems* (SELP systems). If you are reading this then you are in possession *The Byzantine Pineapple (Part 1)*.

More information can be found by searching the text on the web or by reading various book reviews.

## G. *Essay no. 1: A comparison of the planned* Painless *production to the recent fail of the Ben-Hur remake (abridged)*

The author created a couple of essays for the purpose of explaining how the lack of direct industry experience makes no difference toward the ability to create products that will be global successes. From a marketing perspective, the essays document certain marketing constructs of the products.

The essays are abridged to remove the direct review quotes from IMDB and Rotten Tomatoes. Hey, it beats chasing around the legal issue of "rights" for the reviews. However, if the reader wants, they can visit IMDB and Rotten Tomatoes and confirm that the essays reflect the user commentary. Also, the author can be contacted for a private copy of the unabridged material.

Separately, if any person has followed the major movie studios, then one probably has heard the wailing and gnashing of teeth of movie industry executives over how sites such as Rotten Tomatoes supposedly kill movie box office because unfair critics post how bad the newly released products suck and how the populace doesn't go pay for the movies at the theaters. These executives seem to think that the products they have created really aren't as sucky as the general public thinks the films are. Once again, the customers are considered to be the problem, not the products.

The humorous aspect is that movie industry executives pay lots of money continuously for marketing surveys to be performed. Yet all the information required about what the public thinks and wants is all available for free on the review websites! The reviews—legit reviews and not movie-industry-planted reviews—provide all the information about what the public really thinks without paying for surveys!

# CONTENTS

# 1. Introduction

A prior question has been raised about the experience in the industry of Bill Poje and, inherently, the rest of those involved with Corporation X. Industry experience is interpreted strictly in the movie industry context, although there are other industries that this could be applied to, such as bookselling and merchandising and all the inherent activities involved with these industries (e.g., potentially collecting production funds from movie tie-ins, such as from the State of Florida Tourism for a tie-in with the actors/actresses as the *Painless* / the Less trilogy products are intentionally designed to be sold for tourism in Florida).

As prior replies have noted, there are many facets to the question posed. It so happens that August 19, 2016, saw the release of the sixth cinematic version of *Ben-Hur*. This essay compares certain aspects of this latest *Ben-Hur* production to the proposed *Painless* cinematic project to further detail that both the relevant business experience is possessed by Bill Poje / Corporation X staff and also, again, that having movie industry experience doesn't guarantee making good business decisions.

The information for this analysis comes from public data available on the internet, specifically the following:

a. The Numbers website with *Ben-Hur* web page as well as production company pages for MGM, Paramount Pictures, Lightworkers Media, and the Sean Daniel Company
b. Rotten Tomatoes website with *Ben-Hur* page
c. IMDB website with *Ben-Hur* page
d. Wikipedia pages for *Ben-Hur*, Sean Daniel, Mark Burnett, and Timur Bekmambetov
e. Deadline.com article on the poor opening weekend box office of *Ben-Hur*
f. Hollywood Reporter article noting budget information
g. LMN Online noting extent of the financial disaster of *Ben-Hur*

The specific web links to the source material is contained in appendix A. Appendix A is not included in this publication.

The purpose of this essay is not to be critical of the decision-making surrounding *Ben-Hur*, although this obviously occurs. The purpose of this essay is to show that while the senior management of Corporation X may never have worked on a major motion picture, the senior management understands why a product such as *Ben-Hur* would never live up to the internal marketing projections that drove the creation of the product. *Painless*, the Less trilogy, and the other future Corporation X products are specifically designed to avoid the failures of *Ben-Hur*. This essay evidences that Corporation X knows what the Corporation X team is creating and why it will succeed where *Ben-Hur* failed.

# 2. The experience of the Ben-Hur production\ distribution companies\staff

The Wikipedia's *Ben-Hur* page shows that the producers of *Ben-Hur* are Sean Daniel, Mark Burnett, Duncan Henderson, and Joni Levin. The *Ben-Hur* production companies Wiki listed are Sean Daniels Production, Lightworkers Media, and Bazelevs.

If one reviews Sean Daniel's and Mark Burnett's Wiki pages, one can see that these gentlemen have been involved in successful TV and movie productions.

For example, Wiki lists this selected Sean Daniel experience:

> In 1976, he joined Universal Pictures as a film production executive and in 1985, at the age of 34, he became production president, the youngest in the studio's history, a position he held for 5 years. At Universal he supervised the financing and production of such acclaimed films as National Lampoon's Animal House, Coal Miner's Daughter, The Blues Brothers, The Breakfast Club, Sixteen Candles, Fast Times at Ridgemont High, Brazil, Field of Dreams, Do the Right Thing, Back to the Future, Out of Africa,

Midnight Run, Born on the Fourth of July, Missing, Weird Science, Uncle Buck, The Great Outdoors, Born in East LA, Fletch, Gorillas in the Mist, Darkman and Monty Pythons The Meaning of Life.

For Mark Burnett, Wiki lists this selected experience:

> Burnett is the executive producer of eight network television shows / specials and two cable shows: *The Voice and Celebrity Apprentice* (NBC); *Survivor and The People's Choice Awards* (CBS); *Shark Tank, Beyond the Tank*, and *500 Questions* (ABC); *Coupled* (Fox); *America's Greatest Makers* (Turner); and *Lucha Underground* (the El Rey Network).

> Burnett additionally produced the cable miniseries *The Bible* and *A.D. The Bible Continues*, as well as the feature films *Son of God, Little Boy*, and *Woodlawn*.

> He has won eight Emmy Awards, four Producers Guild of America Awards, five Critics' Choice Television Awards, and six People's Choice Awards.

The *Deadline* article states the following:

> So as not to alienate faith-based moviegoers, which was the case with Noah veering greatly from the Old Testament, MGM, and Paramount made a point to hire The Bible shepherds Mark Burnett and Roma Downey as EPs.

So MGM and Paramount green-lighted *Ben-Hur* and brought in the executive producers. There are a variety of cooks in the kitchen.

As per the Hollywood Reporter, MGM put up 80 percent of the budget:

> MGM partnered with Paramount in making *Ben-Hur* and put up 80 percent of the financing. Overseas, the epic rolled out in about a third of the marketplace, grossing $10.7

million for a global start of $22 million. It performed best in Mexico and Brazil.

Before MGM green-lighted funding 80 percent of the *Ben-Hur* budget, it is very likely that the marketing department and executive management looked at a variety of marketing data available to reach the funding decision. The movie industry constantly surveys people to determine "what is hot" and to determine "what thespians to cast," as well as other data such as "what marketing tie-ins with major corporations can be inked."

Without seeing the numbers, it can still be stated with near 100 percent certainty that at a minimum, the internal target gross revenue was at least two times the total cost of the marketing and production costs. If the marketing numbers didn't show such values, then why even bother to make the investment in the first place? If the marketing numbers didn't show such a value and the decision was made to move forward, then the decision-making at the studio really leaves something to be desired!

The director of *Ben-Hur* is Timur Bekmambetov. Wiki cited the following:

> In 2004, Bekmambetov wrote and directed *Night Watch* (2004), a popular Russian fantasy film based on the book by Sergey Lukyanenko. The film was extremely successful in Russia and, at the time, became its highest-grossing release ever, making US $16.7 million in Russia alone, more than *The Lord of the Rings: The Fellowship of the Ring*. The sequel to *Night Watch*, *Day Watch* (2006), was likewise written and directed by Bekmambetov. The two films attracted the attention of Fox Searchlight Pictures, which paid $4 million to acquire worldwide distribution rights (excluding Russia and the Baltic states).

> Bekmambetov followed up *Day Watch* with the *The Irony of Fate 2* (2007). This sequel to the famous Soviet film *The Irony of Fate* (1971) is one of the most successful in Russian history, second only to Avatar in total box office receipts.

Bekmambetov's Hollywood directorial debut, *Wanted* (2008), an action blockbuster about a secret society of assassins, was based on a comic-book miniseries of the same name created by Mark Millar and J. G. Jones.

Bekmambetov has also produced a number of films in the US and Russia. *9* (2009), the story of a rag doll in a postapocalyptic world, was directed by Shane Acker and produced by Bekmambetov, Tim Burton, and Jim Lemley. Bekmambetov also produced the action movie *Black Lightning* (2009), the first Russian-language superhero film, with Universal Pictures.

Essentially, then, some very experienced movie/entertainment industry people were involved with the creation of *Ben-Hur*. The industry people have the marketing and production and financing capabilities to really create something special to wow the public and make a fortune.

Since "industry experience" is so critical, then it must be impossible for the *Ben-Hur* production to be anything but one of the top-grossing films of the year. With such experience managing the product, how could it not be?

What in the world could possibly go wrong?

# 3. Budget comparisons

The Numbers website list the *Ben-Hur* production budget as $95 million. The IMDB website lists the production budget as $100 million. Of course, these are not actuals, but the issue is that the *Ben-Hur* production budget values approximate the current production budget estimate of *Painless*, which is $75 million. The point is that the known production budget of *Ben-Hur* and the current estimated production budget of *Painless* are comparable.

The gap between the two budgets closes when one factors out the estimated costs of the screenplay and producer costs of the *Ben-Hur* budget. A reasonable assumption is that the screenplay and producer fees in the *Ben-Hur* budget are a combined minimum of $5 million but, in reality, are probably in excess of a combined $10 million. The *Painless* project doesn't include any costs for these two items because there is no need to add those costs in. Both Poje and Corporation X staff can wait because everyone expects to make money off the *Painless* movie.

As Corporation X's plan G notes, the basic distribution company take is 50 percent of the global box office (GBO). Excluding all other factors (marketing costs plus ancillary product revenue), a product must generate a GBO to production cost multiple of two to *start* breaking even.

The Numbers website shows that *Ben-Hur* is the second film for the Sean Daniel Production Company. The first release was the 2013 mild success *The Best Man Holiday*, which GBO ($72 million) grossed 4.2 times the production budget ($17 million).

The Numbers website shows that *Ben-Hur* is the second film for Lightworkers Media. The first release was the 2014 mild success *Son of God*, which global box office ($71 million) grossed 3.2 times the production budget ($22 million).

Bazelevs Production Company is a Russian company owned by the director. The Numbers does not list any production credits for this firm.

The Numbers website lists that Paramount Pictures has fourteen releases for 2016. *Ben-Hur* is the ninth product released and is currently the fourth most expensive product listed so far in 2016, trailing the new *Star Trek* (budget is $185 million, GBO is $215 million, multiple equal to 1.16), new *Teenage Mutant Ninja Turtles* (budget is $135 million, GBO is $239 million, multiple equal to 1.77), and the October 2016 new *Jack Reacher* (Tom Cruise) movie release (budget is $96 million).

The Numbers website lists that in 2016, MGM has released four films. *Ben-Hur* costs more to make than the other three films' budgets combined.

It is impossible to know the internal expectation of the GBO for *Ben-Hur,* but the product certainly seems to be a signature 2016 release for all the industry-experienced people involved with producing the product. The budget is greater than the production budgets for the prior Sean Daniel Production / Lightworkers Media releases combined. Paramount budgeted as much for *Ben-Hur* as for the new Tom Cruise. MGM budgeted more on *Ben-Hur* than all other 2016 MGM products combined. It is doubtful that these industry-experienced people had anything but, as already noted, a GBO projection under $300 million as a starting point for internal budgeting.

## 4. What does a $95 million (and inherently a Painless $75 million) budget buy?

A $95-million budget buys many items:

a.  **A name director**
b.  **Big-name actors (Tom Cruise, Morgan Freeman)**
c.  **Multinational shooting locations**

IMDB lists four locations for *Ben-Hur:*

- Matera, Basilicata, Italy
- Cinecittà Studios, Cinecittà, Rome, Lazio, Italy
- Painted Canyons, Mecca Hills, California, USA
- (Second-unit filming location)
- Gravina di Puglia, Bari, Apulia, Italy

IMDB lists three locations for the new *Jack Reacher* film, and the locations were obviously chosen for movie tax credit reasons:

- New Orleans, Louisiana, USA
- Louisiana, USA
- USA

What does this mean for a *Painless* $75 million movie production?

1. A quality director and crew can be hired.
2. Quality-name actors/actresses can be hired.
3. Shooting on location throughout Florida and in Michigan and Philadelphia can be achieved.

### d. Big signature scenes

*Ben-Hur* features a ten-to-fifteen-minute chariot race at the end of the movie (different sources use different times). The Wiki links provide a nice five-paragraph summary of how the chariot race was filmed. *Ben-Hur* also features a galley being attacked by Greek warships (anyone who knows anything about Kevin Costner's *Waterworld* costs overruns knows that filing on water can be a very dicey exercise).

What does this mean for a *Painless* $75-million movie production?

The budget should be available to shoot the five major *Painless* signature scenes (page 100).

### e. Top-quality filming production

As Wiki notes, "It will be released in regular 2-D, IMAX, 3-D, Digital 3-D, RealD 3-D, and IMAX 3-D."

What does this mean for a *Painless* $75 million movie production?

*Painless* can be produced in the same manner.

**Contrasting the select data to the Painless project from another perspective:**

*Ben-Hur* has a run time of 124 minutes; *Painless* is estimated at 150 minutes.

*Ben-Hur* has the two main signature action scenes noted above. *Painless* has five signature action scenes (one at eight minutes, three at nine minutes, one at eleven minutes, and the climax at seventeen minutes).

Besides studio locations, *Painless* would be shot on location in South Florida—a car chase from Cocoa to Cocoa Beach, Florida, a two-stage car chase through Detroit, and a climax in San Destin, Florida, with a hurricane destroying the region.

*Painless* currently doesn't have actors/actresses or a director lined up, but with a $75 million budget and five signature action sequences, one can pretty well assume that the experienced people required will flock to the production. The production will be about as big as anything Paramount or MGM are involved in, and the opportunity to get in on such a large production is severely limited on an annual basis. The opinion of everyone involved with Corporation X is that there are plenty of incredibly talented actors/actresses/production staff who are starving for an opportunity such as *Painless*.

It is also interesting to note that with the exception of Morgan Freeman, there are no big household names involved in acting in *Ben-Hur*. Evidently, the industry-experienced management in charge of production did not deem big household names as necessary to achieve box office success. But they still spent $100 million to make *Ben-Hur* even without the big names!

Certainly, everyone involved with Corporation X would like to provide a more detailed budget than the estimated $75 million *Painless* movie production budget. Indeed, every day that passes, some more work is being put forth creating the more detailed production budget. Better capitalization would speed up the process.

Regardless, at this point in time, the Corporation X opinion is that the $75 million budget is a valid estimate for a *Painless* movie production budget. This estimate is based on the manufacturing experience that the Corporation X senior management does possess:

1. Building larger manufacturing facilities for production larger than a *Painless* movie production
2. Performing cash management for manufacturing facilities larger than a *Painless* movie production
3. Budgeting and timely and accurate monthly, quarterly, and annual financial statements and variance reporting for manufacturing facilities larger than a *Painless* movie production
4. Operating payroll/accounting systems for manufacturing facilities larger than a *Painless* movie production
5. Meeting all audit / human resource / government activities for manufacturing facilities larger than a *Painless* movie production
6. Designing/implementing larger information systems' hardware and software for manufacturing facilities larger than a *Painless* movie production
7. Successfully working with human resources hired to maximize human resource usage

The Corporation X senior management is also accustomed to making profit from the larger manufacturing facilities.

# 5. What do the reviews and box office receipts for Ben-Hur show?

Note: Since the release of *Ben-Hur* is so new, the exact numbers cited on any website may change from what is written into this text. No significant change is expected as the numbers roll in.

Among the marketing events that occurred, Wiki notes the following:

The trailer garnered polarized reception from critics and audiences with comparisons being made to *300: Rise of an Empire, Gladiator*, and *Spartacus: Blood and Sand*. In its first week, the trailer was viewed over 8.2 million times across YouTube and Facebook, making it the fourth most viewed trailer of the week. The trailer was also screened in front of over 30,000 people at Hillsong Conference 2016.

Viewers of 8.2 million saw the trailer on YouTube, and undoubtedly, a few million more viewings of the full trailer occurred in movie houses across the USA before their feature film was played. Did this translate into box office success?

News Articles

### The Deadline Article Says It All

With an estimated production cost that's in the vicinity of $100M, MGM and Paramount certainly didn't build *Ben-Hur* to fail this weekend.

### The Hollywood Reporter

Younger moviegoers had virtually no interest in seeing *Ben-Hur*. According to MGM and Paramount, 95 percent of the audience was over the age of 25. The movie skewed slightly female (51 percent).

(Wait! What? Weren't younger moviegoers the target market? How could such industry-experienced experts completely fail to attract the target market with spending $100 million to attract the target market?)

### Variety

*These days, though, notorious movie bombs tend to arrive with an impersonal, disaster-by-committee feeling*

"Ben-Hur" derailed spectacularly at the multiplexes this weekend, as the latest attempt to revive the chariot racing epic opened to an anemic $11.4 million. That's a disastrous result for the $100 million production, putting "Ben-Hur" in the ranks of the summer's biggest flops.

"This is the bomb of the summer," said Jeff Bock, a box office analyst with Exhibitor Relations. "They went big and they went home."

Although MGM put up roughly 80% of the budget for the film, its failure will be felt at Paramount. The studio has had a bad streak at the box office of late, fielding duds such as *Teenage Mutant Ninja Turtles: Out of the Shadows* and *Zoolander 2*.

The film, it seems, could not expand beyond its core Christian audience.

As always, there are lessons to be gleaned from the carnage. Here are five reasons why *Ben-Hur* crashed and burned:

- **Critics hated it.**
- **The kids didn't show up.**
- **Swords and sandals epics were falling flat.**
- **Marketing was muddled.**
- **Audiences craved something fresh.**

### LMN Online

But how much of a disaster was Ben-Hur, given that it's already being coined as perhaps the biggest flop of the year?

As we know, the film was made on a budget that ran north of $100 million, and in its opening weekend, it only managed to recoup $11.2 million, a little more than one-tenth of its budget. Keep in mind, this doesn't even take into account the cost of marketing, and as a general rule of thumb marketing cost usually matches pretty closely to the overall budget of a picture (e.g., we can likely expect the marketing budget of this one to be $100 million, making the overall cost of the film $200 million—in theory), though of course this is only a rule of thumb, not a law. But all in all, rival studios put the break-even point for Ben-Hur at around $250 million worldwide.

Given the lackluster opening, THR speculates that Ben-Hur will ultimately end its theater run at around $30 million, still only about one-third of its budget, and less than one-sixth of its overall costs (and this isn't even taking into account that the studio doesn't see 100% of the money from ticket sales). All in all, it looks to have been a bad investment for Paramount Pictures and MGM, and rival studios believe when all said and done, the film w lose $100 million.

THR is quick to point out that sources close to the film believe that the number is closer to $60 million or $75 million, once you take home releases into account.

## Summary

What went wrong? Some will argue the subject matter, but Mel Gibson's *The Passion of the Christ* had a GBO of $370 million in 2004. Also, if the subject matter is so questionable, then why did the industry experts invest the human and financial resources they did to make such a turkey? And if industry experience is so important, then how could the industry experts have screwed up?

The author once saw an interview with Arnold Schwarzenegger talking about his bomb *The Last Action Hero*. What Arnold basically stated was "We all read the script and thought it was great. Then we made the movie. Then we watched the movie and were horrified by how horrible it was. Then we had to go sell it to the public."

It's a pretty safe bet that everyone involved with *Ben-Hur* felt something similar as they watched the initial *Ben-Hur* screening.

The bottom line is that despite all the industry experience and major budget available, the production management really didn't know before production just what they were making. If they did, they never would have made it in the first place!

# 6. The review details document what is wrong with Ben-Hur

According to Rotten Tomatoes, *Ben-Hur* has a 29 percent critics rating and a 66 percent audience rating for both groups liking it. The IMDB rating is 5.2 out of 10. With numbers like these, it is doubtful that *Ben-Hur* will be anything but a major financial loss. (Note: all review data was collected on Monday, August 22, 2016. This was the Monday after the opening weekend.)

The seven items in categories *a* to *g* below are what the IMDB and Rotten Tomatoes reviews generally indicate is wrong with *Ben-Hur*. The reviews that note the items are listed with the cross-reference to the review in the appendices. The evidence of items *a* to *g* is demonstrated in the various review snippets posted in appendix B and C.

After the first weekend, there were thirty-five reviews (IMDB reviews) and the quotes in appendix B are from fourteen (40 percent) of the reviews. It is telling that after the opening weekend, only thirty-five reviews are posted; most major films have over two hundred reviews by this time. People just don't care.

The IMDB and RT numbers correspond to the review number in the appendices that document the relevant section.

a. A disjointed climax with too much shaky cam, making it too hard to figure out what is going on. This is coupled with animal brutality that will stop many people from repeating as customers.

This is particularly humorous in light of the Wiki quotes from the director about his choice of shooting technique for the grand finale:

> Bekmambetov's goal was to shoot these action scenes so realistically that the audience feels that they're in the chariot, driving. He was inspired by YouTube videos and Instagram photos, "The camerawork is very specific when we see Nascar or motorbike racing on YouTube. It's either long-lens (close-up) cameras, very professional, or it's iPhone cameras from people in the crowd, cars passing by at the speed of light, and they barely have a chance to pan and catch something.

D'oh!

IMDB: 7
RT: 1, 4, 5, 6, 8, 12, 13, 14, 15, 20, 24, 28, 34, 37, 38, 42, 44

b.  Poor cinematography wherein many scenes are too dark and too much use of close-ups instead of panoramic view for the chariot race.

IMDB: 8
RT: 4, 5, 13, 24, 42, 44

c.  Poor script construct, making for choppy storytelling, necessitating voice-overs, and having little character development.

All fourteen of the IMDB reviews selected note this problem!

IMDB: 1, 2, 3, 4, 5, 6, 7, 8, 9, 10, 11, 12, 13, 14
RT: 1, 2, 4, 5, 6, 9, 10, 11, 13, 14, 16, 17, 18, 19, 20, 21, 22, 23, 24, 25, 26, 27, 28, 29, 30, 32, 33, 35, 36, 39, 40, 43

d.  Poor dialogue.

    IMDB: 6, 7, 10, 11, 12
    RT: 1, 2, 4, 5, 6, 8, 9, 10, 13, 14, 16, 17, 18, 19, 20, 21, 22, 30, 33, 35, 36, 39, 40

e.  Miscast actors who do not connect with the audience.

    IMDB: 6, 10, 11, 13
    RT: 1, 2, 4, 5, 10, 12, 13, 14, 16, 19, 24, 30, 31, 39, 40

f.  Morgan Freeman is good, but he also "mailed it in." (An opinion is that Morgan Freeman knew he was part of a turkey and just couldn't muster the enthusiasm.)

    IMDB: 5
    RT: 1, 4, 16, 18, 24

g.  A sense of lack of purpose of why the film is being made other than to create the chariot race at the end of the film. This also leads into the muddled attempt at conveying a religious message. The combination leads to marketing to a limited target market of faith-based youth. PG rating and a chariot race at the end that the *Deadline* article states is marketed incorrectly:

    Faith-based insiders criticize a majority of *Ben-Hur*'s spots for focusing too heavily on the chariot race. (One criticized them as being too "Jesus meets *Fast & Furious*.")

    IMDB: 7
    RT: 2, 3, 4, 5, 6, 7, 10, 13, 14, 17, 22, 27, 28, 29, 31, 34, 35, 36, 40, 41, 43, 44

# 7. How Painless differs from the 2016 Ben-Hur Part 1: Review issues

A. The first two segments of the review issues (*A* and *B*) noted focus on the camera work for the chase scene and the cinematography being poor. These issues roll into the same issue: poor decisions about director hiring and vision with what and how you are presenting and why it will (or will not!) work with the public.

Corporation X's plan G, page 12, has a *Painless* movie timing schedule plus the producer is the screenwriter. There is also the three DVD sets of a prototype Less trilogy film production. The novel *Painless* is basically the screenplay as the novel was written with all the dialogue for the screenplay. The *Painless* management has a clear understanding of what product is to be produced.

The product is designed to have the visuals of *The Godfather* parts 1 and 2. The characters are dressed nicely and show a variety of emotions. The scenery changes, and the color palette also changes.

The romance, spice, and steam is designed to draw on aspects of *Desperate Housewives*. There is soap opera and steam, and when people watch the men and women, their libido is stirred. The viewers also like the dual injection of deviousness and humor into the characters. The characters get to be over-the-top in a sexy, delightfully dangerous manner built with foreplay to a climax.

The two car chase scenes are designed to use the environment of the chases. The Detroit chase is designed to use both wealthy and poor areas—suburb, inner city, industrial, Tiger's home opener, and Downtown Detroit. The Cocoa to Cocoa Beach chase uses three bridges and both natural and small city elements, as well as locations such as the Cape Canaveral Hospital. The visuals to be presented are threefold combo: panorama, action between vehicles, and action in vehicles. The base model is the chase scene from *Bullitt*.

An overriding theme is that the viewer can always see what is going on! The reviews note that the chariot race is incomprehensible because you can't see what is going on because of the shaky cam. The *Painless* production doesn't want that. Just because you *can* show an *X* games or video games' perspective doesn't mean that you *should* show that perspective. Watch the Matrix trilogy. There is plenty of action, with no shaky cam, and one can pretty well see the action and what is occurring.

A second overriding theme is the editing and evolution of the chase flow. The movie *Salt* has a New York City chase where the vehicles doing the chasing stopped through New York City traffic, alternating from being on the left side of the road to the right side of the road and then back to the left side of the road! The flow/continuity makes no sense.

The *Painless* chases are designed to use all the wide lanes and the natural environment. The viewer is to be taken along for the ride in a manner that upholds "suspension of disbelief." Chase flow and panorama, as well as closer continuity that can be followed on screen, will not be an issue.

When the time comes to interview directors (the directors obviously have read the story preinterview), the process will be to use the Corporation X–timing schedule and to walk through all eighty-four segments with respect to what and how the product is to be created. There will not be any confusion between producer and director as to what is being created because if there are disagreements as to the why, what, and how of every segment to be created, these disagreements will be obvious during the interview process. If there is no agreement, there will be no hiring. (Inherently, this same process extends to the primary actors/actresses to be hired. If they don't get the vision, they will not be casted.)

B. The second two segments of the reviews (*C* and *D*) noted focus on the poor script construction and poor dialogue. If one thinks about it, this is quite stunning. The screenplay writers and everyone else involved took a story that was an amazing best seller and the subject for two of the greatest Hollywood financial successes and managed to turn it into a jumbled mess with this reenvisioning. It takes talent to really bollix up a great story, but *Ben-Hur* is proof that it can be done.

*Painless* / the Less trilogy and all the other Poje works intended for film or stage are, in many ways, a direct reaction from watching and reading twenty years of declining story-writing and product creation. This led to the realization that there is a huge market void for the following:

1. Original products that are well-constructed in the respect that there are fully developed characters who look and act like normal human beings and who have interpersonal relationships like modern human beings have rather than some simplistic two-dimensional comic book–style presentation of characters. The characters have a past as well as logical reasons for their actions. They act like adults.

2. Original products that are not filled with dialogue that sounds like the text was from the first or second draft scripting and then the writers decided to stop at that point because to really make the people sound human requires really working the dialogue through more times. It means mentally putting oneself in the theatre, watching and listening to the dialogue being spoken and being able to

know what lines will really sound stupid to people and which lines will not.

*Painless* is available for reading; so are all the *Painless* book reviews. To quote the *Writer's Digest* review: "Your second strength is in your ability to capture real-to-life dialogue. The conversations had a ring of truth to them."

3. Original products that are in a modern-time setting and reflects the lives of people in America today. Aug and Jocelyn are constructed to be a metaphoric form of Mr. and Mrs. America. Their relationship embodies many of the aspects people in America have to deal with daily while still providing escapist fantasy.

The movie timing schedule exists for *Painless*. The three DVD prototypes are available for viewing. Poje is available for discussion on these three topics in terms of not only *Painless* but also the rest of the Less trilogy, as well as other products. Resources are available that will prove the three scripting and dialogue points listed. All one has to do is to avail themselves of the resources.

C. The third two segments of the reviews (*E* and *F*) noted focus on miscast characters or a big-name actor mailing it in. As already noted with the director's interview process, the cast interview process will entail going through every segment of the product and discussing the details of the why, what, and how of every segment to get the cast who *are* properly cast and who *won't* mail it in.

D. The last set of reviews ask this question: Why did anyone even make this movie? People who watch the movie really don't know after watching *Ben-Hur*.

*Painless* / the Less trilogy are about how people in America live. Aug and Jocelyn love each other, but their whole relationship is built on lies. The media and the government and the political parties and the corporations all have relationships with the citizens, but much of the relationships are built on lies. An opinion is that if the reader does not see this, then the reader is not seeing what the common people of America (and the rest of the world who look up to America for leadership) see and experience daily.

Therefore, for the international market/marketing, *Painless* / the Less trilogy is about America. It is the America the common people was told through entertainment that is showcased for the viewers to enjoy and think about.

All these are done using exciting signature scenes featuring car chases, erotic steam in a car, soap opera, select violence, and a major hurricane finish. The hurricane finish is metaphor of America today, where the chase of riches occurs by people seemingly oblivious to the hurricane swirling around outside them.

In other words, *Painless* / the Less trilogy have a purpose. This purpose will resonate with consumers globally.

# 8. How Painless differs from the 2016 Ben-Hur Part 2: Other issues

There are other significant differences between *Painless* / the Less trilogy and *Ben-Hur*:

a.   *Target market*

The target market for *Ben-Hur* is a combination of youth (PG rating and extreme-sport, shaky-cam realism) and religious people. This is a very limited market base to shoot for. As the reviews show, *Ben-Hur* seems to bore many viewers to get to the chase scenes. The reviews show that the evangelical scripting is also trite and boring. Also, as the news articles point out, people under twenty-five years old are staying away (so much for knowing their target market).

The target market for *Painless* is adults globally. The *R* rating is not a concern to draw audiences, and the suspicion is that there will be plenty of fifteen-to-eighteen-year-olds who will end up being chaperoned to the theatre.

If you think the target market is too broad, then stop a second and ask yourself whether movies such as *The GodFather*, the Matrix trilogy, *Avatar*, etc. are popular with a limited target market or whether it is the broad appeal that made the films a theater and posttheater success. The answer is obvious: unless one gets broad support from males and females in all marketing demographics, then one won't have a smash success. It really is that simple.

b. *Run time of the product / character development*

*Ben-Hur* runs just over two hours and the planned run time of *Painless* is two and a half hours. The primary reason for the extra half hour of *Painless* run time is that this time is used to develop the characters. How many of the *Ben-Hur* reviews noted a choppy script and illogical story? Quite a few.

The reason for the *Ben-Hur* specific time length is partially a result of creating a product not to show a story but rather show an abridged story to fit a specific time length. Inherently, this means that the length of the product to be shown in theaters is more important than the story or the coherence of the final product.

The year 1968 saw the release of Sergio Leone's *Once Upon a Time in the West*. The film initially bombed in America and became a smash hit in Europe. Why? Wikipedia quoted,

The original version by the director was 166 minutes (2 hours and 46 minutes) when it was first released on December 21, 1968. This was the version that was to be shown in European cinemas and was a box office success. For the US release on May 28, 1969, *Once Upon a Time in the West* was edited down to 145 minutes (2 hours and 25 minutes) by Paramount and was a financial flop. The film is now generally acknowledged as a masterpiece and one of the greatest films ever made. In 2009, the film was selected for preservation in the United States National Film Registry by the Library of Congress as being culturally, historically, or aesthetically significant. (https://en.wikipedia. org/wiki/Once_Upon_a_Time_in_the_West)

The original US release of *Once Upon a Time in the West* had a twenty-one-minute cut, creating a choppy product that viewers could not follow or understand. In 1968, some experienced movie studio / distribution executives watched what is now arguably one of the greatest films ever made, and then they decided to edit out twenty-one minutes solely to have a shorter run time. These experienced executives favored a shorter run time to try and get more daily viewings in the theater. Instead, by making that decision, these experienced executives took a financial hit and turned it into a loss.

The story takes as long as it takes to show. By cutting the novel of *Ben-Hur* down, the creators of the product also cut down the story and cut down the box office take.

c. *Time period of the story*

*Ben-Hur* takes place in AD 33. *Painless* primarily takes place in 2005, with backstory scenes from 1978 forward occurring.

This is a huge difference in production. In *Ben-Hur,* every scene must have all the sets, wardrobe, etc. settings recreated to simulate a time two thousand years ago. Quite a few reviews note out-of-place clothing and that all characters amazingly having straight white teeth. A lot of money was spent on wardrobe and sets to match the time period two thousand years ago, yet no one thought that the teeth are a part of make-up and wardrobe. Part of the reason of missing this facet is because 100 percent of everything from two thousand years ago has to be recreated and everyone missed thinking about this aspect.

This also means that most of the film production looks like the sand color noted in select reviews. This means that the color palate of the film didn't change for the daytime land scenes. The viewer sees the same imagery over and over again. Reviews note that the entire film looks like it went through multiple "bleachings" to get a sandy look. This created a generic color palette that dulls the viewer.

What is somewhat humorous about that aspect is that if every frame of *Ben-Hur* is whitewashed multiple times, then they could have spent time digitally coloring the characters' teeth at the same time. Obviously, this did not occur.

In *Painless,* it is not necessary to recreate a prior time period for the entire two-and-a-half-hour product. Creating the 1980 Detroit setting and car chase and 1980 Detroit Tiger home opener will present some costly challenges but certainly no more of a challenge than digitally recreating a coliseum and a chariot race. But the overall *Painless* production is specifically designed to be much simpler with respect to sets, wardrobe, and all the other little details that must be accounted for to properly simulate ancient times.

*Painless* is also designed for many color changes. The film isn't meant to bore people with a repetitive color tone throughout the viewing time.

d. *Strong female lead character*

*Ben-Hur* has *no* strong female characters. The *Ben-Hur* reviews state that the female roles are undeveloped and given short shrift. Guess what? Females aren't going to be as interested in a story without strong female characters, so the *Ben-Hur* production alienates 50 percent of the moviegoing public.

*Painless* not only has the strong lead of Jocelyn but also Aug's first wife, Laurie, as well as the mothers of Aug, Jocelyn, and Angel being developed. Not only are the characters developed, but also the various romantic triangles are developed. It was a concept ignored by *Ben-Hur*. *Painless* is designed to bring the female audience to the theater.

e. *Steamy scenes*

The *Ben-Hur* reviews note nothing about stimulating erotic scenes in the movie. This makes sense as the film shortchanges the female characters, and according to the reviews, it seems to focus on the two major action scenes to the detriment of all else.

*Painless* is designed to stimulate the libido of the viewing audience. The construct is designed to generate repeat business because the viewers enjoy the sexual stimulation/arousal that sections of the film are designed to elicit from the viewing audience.

f.  *Proper use of violence*

The reviews for *Ben-Hur* note that the violence in the movie is pushed to the PG rating extreme. The chariot race is noted for bodies being run over and mangled and for horses being whipped and beaten. Ask yourself this question: How many people do you think will want to repeatedly watch horses being beaten via repeat viewership? Not many that this author knows.

*Painless* certainly has violence built in, but the scenes of violence are primarily quick and not overtly gruesome enough to turn stomachs. *Painless* is designed so that the violence is mostly humans fighting humans (without lengthy gun battles) or of a car chase variety. Animal beating/violence is not part of the script.

g.  *Using the end of the film in the beginning and the use of voice-overs and time placards to move the story forward*

Ask yourself this question: Have you ever heard the phrase "Show me, don't tell me"? In writing and in film, the difference between a schlock product and an excellent product is usually the script and poor dialogue and telling people the story. Usually telling the story with bad dialogue is a kiss of death.

The reviews indicate that the start of *Ben-Hur* is the chariot race. Then the movie is flash backed in time. This tells the viewer the end long before it is time for the end. Why has the story been constructed and the film edited this way? Generally, this is an indication that there is a lack of confidence of the "meat of the story" being strong enough to carry viewer interest. The exciting or dramatic point of climax is initially shown in an abridged version in the belief that this will hold the viewer's attention. Seasoned movie viewers are now familiar with this gimmick and take this as a sign of more of the same to come.

The reviews indicate that there are voice-overs by Morgan Freeman to tell the viewer what has happened. This saves time at the expense of character development.

The reviews indicate that there are various points in the movie where the location and year/date are flashed on the screen. This is easy to do to tell the viewer the time and location. What is lost is the subtlety of showing the viewers the location and year/date relevant through showing the story.

All three screenplay-writing techniques (using the end in the beginning, using voice-overs, and using time and location placards) are generally indications of lazy writing. All three techniques are telling the story. The way to write a story is to show the story. Very few stories effectively use one or more of the three techniques.

None of the Poje works/screenplays use these techniques. The written material is worked over to craft a compelling story that shows what is occurring through the characters.

For example, the opening day of *Painless* is July 19, 2005. It is extremely easy to put up a time and date stamp to show this to the audience. Instead, the story is constructed so that there is shipping paperwork and documents to be signed to show what date it is. There is also discussion of the recent Roger Mayweather fight, which also specifically locates the time and date through showing the viewer the date and time versus telling the viewer with obviousness.

# 9. Conclusion

*Ben-Hur* is neither the first nor the last big-budget Hollywood financial flop. It is merely another in a long line of forgettable financial fiascos that the Hollywood entertainment industry continues to annually pump out in growing numbers. For all the money spent on celebrity buildup and market surveying and all the experience possessed by the Hollywood executives, they annually have been and continued to make boneheaded product (and inherently financial) decisions.

According to the MGM Holdings, financial statements ending December 31, 2012 (http://www.mgm.com/about/pdfview.php?id=1), the stock options issued in 2011 was $21 million and in 2012 was $16 million for a combined $37 million. The lion's share of this compensation undoubtedly went to the executives of MGM Holdings and is probably consistent at a minimum of $15 million annually. These stock options are in excess of direct compensation and other executive perks.

The compensation for Paramount Pictures' executives is not publicly available. It can be assumed that the compensation for the Paramount executives is similar to MGM Holdings.

Certainly, the corporate executives have more than just one product produced and more activities than just film production. Both studios have also experienced some megahit over the years as well as other financial failures. Sometimes, they do get it right.

That said, MGM stands to directly lose upward of $80+ million on *Ben-Hur*. Indirectly, the loss is even greater because the idea is to make money on a film release, and there is no accounting for lost profit in the analysis.

Paramount Pictures stands to lose $25+ million on *Ben-Hur*. This value can be coupled with the estimated $100+ million lost in 2016 on the latest *Star Trek* movie, as well as another $50+ million lost in 2016 on the latest *Teenage Mutant Ninja Turtles* movie. Again, there is no accounting for lost profit in the analysis.

It seems to be that the industry executives at both corporations are being paid millions to lose hundreds of millions. So much for industry experience!

As stated in the introduction, the purpose of this essay is to show that while the senior management of Corporation X may never have worked on a major motion picture, the senior management understands why a product such as *Ben-Hur* would never live up to the internal marketing projections that drove the creation of the product. It's up to the reader to decide who they think knows more about using ultimately a $75 million dollar production investment to create a movie with a minimum $300 million global box office and potentially much greater global box office.

The people green-lighting products such as *Ben-Hur* or the people who have the *Painless* product (and more products) ready to go?

## H. *Essay no. 2: A comparison of the planned* Painless *production to the recent fail of* The Sea of Trees

# CONTENTS

# 1. Introduction

This essay compares the $25 million independent film flop *The Sea of Trees* to the proposed Corporation X *Painless,* the Less trilogy, and other ten years of already-planned projects for the corporation. The purpose of this essay is to demonstrate that the marketing construct of *Painless* is well-thought-out and will achieve the financial targets whereas *The Sea of Trees* marketing was not well-thought-out for product design and marketing, which means that the project had a $25 million loss from day 1.

This essay can be considered to be a sequel to the prior essay comparing *Painless* to the financial flop of *Ben-Hur*. The construct is similar: first, going through the people behind *The Sea of Trees*; then review summaries, a comparison of "what went wrong" to why *Painless* will be a success; and finally, a conclusion.

The information cited comes from public sources. As in the prior essay, the reference website links and review snippets are presented in appendices following the text.

# 2. The experience of The Sea of Trees production/ distribution companies/staff

Per Wiki and the Numbers, *The Sea of Trees* was produced by three different groups: Bloom, Gil Netter Productions, and Waypoint Entertainment. The film is an independent production.

The 2014 *Deadline* article provides details on the financing:

> The original Essay contains a link and excerpt from
> Deadline.com that notes The Sea of Trees as a title that
> should draw interest. The author would like to have printed
> the link and excerpt from Deadline.com but 3 emails over a
> one month period to 4 editors at Deadline.com were never

responded to for assistance to get authorization to reprint the Deadline.com material.

So *The Sea of Trees* is the first Bloom project.

The Numbers website shows that Waypoint Enterprises produced one movie in 2011 and has four releases in 2016. This may be technically correct, but *The Sea of Trees* was actually premiered at the Cannes Film festival in 2015. According to the Numbers, *The Nice Guys* by Waypoint has a global box office of $57 million, but IMDB shows that the budget for the film was $50 million, which makes the film about a $25 million loser. *Knight of Cups* has an all-star cast and an Academy Award–nominee director, but the budget is mysteriously unposted on the internet and the global box office is $1.1 million, which means it probably was another financial flop.

Gil Netter Productions, on the other hand, has produced four other movies with three *big* successes: *Marley & Me, The Blind Side, Water for Elephants, and Life of Pi.*

*The Sea of Trees* has an Academy Award–winning director Gus Van Sant and Academy Award–winning actor Matthew McConaughey and Academy Award–nominee Naomi Watts.

What could possibly go wrong?

# 3. Review details document what is wrong with The Sea of Trees

*The Sea of Trees* was entered as a contestant for the Palme d'Or at the Cannes Film Festival. The movie was laughed at and booed in the theater. It took a year to secure a distributor for theater release where the film has tanked basically drawing no one to the theater. What went wrong?

The reviews in the appendices note a few different recurring themes:

1. Terrible script

   IMDB: 4, 5, 8, 9, 10, 11, 12
   RT: 1, 2, 3, 4, 5, 6, 7, 8, 9, 11, 12, 13, 14, 15, 16, 17, 18, 19, 20, 21, 22, 24, 25, 26, 27, 28, 29

2. Terrible dialog

   RT: 1, 2, 4, 5, 8, 10, 11, 13, 14, 15, 17, 19, 23, 26, 27, 29

3. Slow pacing

   IMDB: 5, 7, 10, 13, 14
   RT: 2, 5, 8, 9, 10, 12, 13, 15. 17, 19, 24, 29

4. Terrible music

   RT: 1, 2, 5, 15, 19, 20, 23, 29

The cinematography is noted as nice, but cinematography alone isn't going to get people to the theater or to get them to buy a copy for the home collection or to get people to watch repetitively on TV.

What Makes the Script So Awful, and Why Is Painless Better?

It is the opinion of this author that those who read the script should have known before starting that the script would not bring people to the theater. If one understands the concept of translating what is written on the paper to what people will see on the screen, the faults are obvious.

a. What the audience sees from the main actor

   The run time is 106 minutes (one hour and forty-six minutes). The lead actor is on the screen virtually the entire time. The lead actor is a weepy, whiny (supposedly), suicidal (henpecked) husband. Except when dodging a stormy flood in the forest, what the audience sees for nearly two hours is a weepy, whiny, miserable male. Who wants to spend two hours watching that?

In the prior essay, note was made of the Arnold Schwarzenegger bomb *The Last Action Hero*. The same fundamental flaw existed in that script. For two hours, the audience sees a whiny, snot-nosed kid who most people would rather punch in the face than do anything else with. Who wants to spend two hours doing that?

In *Painless*, protagonists Aug and Jocelyn are not on the screen for the full length of the movie. There are other characters who take their time on the screen. There are three Detroit-area scenes that change the characters and develop the story, as well as action in Philadelphia and Nashville.

Another aspect is that *Painless* mixes the emotions of the characters. For the most part, the imagery presented by the actors/actresses is that of *happy, smiling, devious people*! They aren't happy all the time. They do experience some tragedy, and arguably, the steamy, erotic scenes show a different emotion than happiness. The fight scenes are sometimes mixed with humor, and the tension of a fight, which means different emotions, is shown. The point is that over a two-and-a-half-hour period, a variety of actors/actresses are shown presenting a wide variety of emotions versus one mopey actor for nearly two hours.

b.   The suspension of disbelief

The suspension of disbelief is what keeps an audience involved in the movie. Any flaws in the plot are accepted by the audience who are swept up in the ride rather than losing the audience to thinking this is just absurd.

*The Sea of Trees* reviews detail the beginning of the story: actor drives to airport and has a one-way ticket to Japan to go to the forest where one hundred people kill themselves annually. This is the kind of ridiculous plot contrivance that may suck people in on paper, but when you see it on screen, it just comes off as stupid.

First, as one review notes, in a post-9/11 world, one just doesn't buy a one-way ticket to Japan. Then if such a forest existed and there were one hundred people committing suicide there a year and one is buying a one-way plane ticket to the general area, don't you think red flags would be going off somewhere? That forest would be barricaded by suicide-prevention hotline people!

Worse than that, most people have known someone who has committed suicide, failed an attempt at suicide, or seriously contemplated suicide. Has anyone ever known anyone who was so suicidal despondent and ready to end their own lives that they took the time to book a plane ticket to a foreign country to fly there and kill themselves? D'oh! Besides that, anyone who knows suicide statistics knows that women are way more predisposed than men to kill themselves by either pills or wrist slashing—the two methods chosen by the two male characters in the forest!

From step 1, the suspension of disbelief is completely annihilated! Then there is the rest of the film to go!

*Painless* takes the time to create a believable scenario—believable enough to achieve the suspension of disbelief. The action starts with ocean containers being opened and inspected at an import/export company. Real-life props that are humorous are immediately used: the big black dick products and the plush animals and the Killer Beez amusement game. Jokes are told.

Sexual innuendo and criminal innuendo are used. The audience is entertained versus shown depression.

c.   The action

The reviews state that *The Sea of Trees* is basically a main actor wandering through a forest with an unrealistic, stereotyped sidekick while the main character psychobabbles. The psychobabble is interrupted by flashbacks of an unrealistic couple arguing and reflecting an unrealistic marriage.

Wandering through a forest, babbling for a couple of hours, is boring and needs action to liven up the story, so the answer is to have the characters fall *and* hurt themselves *and* get caught in a storm/flood *and* to take clothes off dead bodies so that they can stay warm! (This does seem to indicate that although the dead bodies are lying in the same forest that was just poured on by rain and also had a flood wash through that the bodies themselves remained dry. The characters also are lucky that the bodies chosen did not relieve themselves after death to soil the clothing! Undoubtedly, the clothes' sizes is also a perfect match). This is coupled with a convenient car crash and a signature scene toward the end of the main character having an exposition on life at a campfire. Be still my beating heart!

It is already documented that *Painless* has five signature scenes that comprise a full hour of chases, romantic steam, fights, and a big hurricane finish! There is a reason that *Painless* has a budget of $50 million greater than *The Sea of Trees*. It costs more money to make the entertaining action, but the payoff is at the global box office plus ancillary sales.

d.   The terrible dialogue

Virtually, every review makes note of how awful the dialogue in *The Sea of Trees* is. The characters simply do not speak like normal human beings. As one review notes, this starts in the very beginning with a phony issue at the airline ticket counter and continues through nearly two hours of the film.

The terrible dialogue contributes to the annihilation of the suspension of disbelief. The unbelievable actions are married with unbelievable dialogue. What do the filmmakers receive out of this marriage? They were laughed at and booed at the Cannes Film Festival!

The first essay already makes a statement as to the validity of the *Painless* dialogue. There is no need to rehash the validity here.

e.   The slow pacing

Many of the reviews note the slow pacing of *The Sea of Trees*. More than one review mentions being so bored during the film that the reviewer mentally started anticipating what will happen as well as counting the volume of other movies ripped off. The viewer interest was not held.

Much of this slow pacing is attributable to the already-noted lack of action. The lack of action is coupled with unnecessary scenes as the reviewer noted superfluous filler scenes, such as the airline attendant fumbling around to try and find the protagonist's missing plane flight reservation. These superfluous scenes are included to lengthen *The Sea of Trees*. The reviewers also note that the marriage scenes repetitively belabor the same troubled-marriage presentation over and over and over. All of the above add up to slow (and boring) pacing.

This can be contrasted to the already-documented varieties of action in *Painless* that comprise an hour of chases, fights, and steam, as well as a hurricane finish. *Painless* is intentionally constructed to keep a faster pace moving the story along in a manner that isn't boring.

f. The music

Quite a few of the reviews note the mismatched music. The music is described as *lachrymose*, which means "slow and weepy." This music permeates the film. The film construct, therefore, is a combination of a weepy lead actor spouting terrible dialogue at a terminally slow pace, coupled with a weepy soundtrack. What a great way to spend nearly two hours!

The orchestra music for *Painless* has yet to be written, but the soundtrack features modern songs that vary in town and are chosen not only for their beat but also because the lyrics match the characters' moods and thoughts. This soundtrack portion features songs by Sweet, the Kinks, the Divinyls, Guns N' Roses, AC/DC, David Bowie, and Faith No More, among other singers/bands. This is definitely not lachrymose music!

# 4. The marketing vision of The Sea Of Trees versus Painless

Ask yourself this question: Who is the target market for *The Sea of Trees*?

Did they expect this to be a date-night movie? Did they expect couples with marital troubles to attend? Did they expect a suicide reversal story to entice adults? They certainly couldn't have expected the film to resonate with the comic book crowd. Just who did they expect to attend?

Ask yourself this question: Who was the marketing tie-in for ancillary products for *The Sea of Trees*?

Did they expect to have a tie-in with Japan Airlines and the Japanese Department of Tourism to run a campaign of "Fly to Japan and see the suicide forest"? That campaign would have failed anyway because the film was shot in Massachusetts instead of in Japan.

Perhaps, they could have an ad for Sanofi-Aventis, which is the manufacturer of Ambien. The ad could read something like "When you want to commit suicide in the Japanese suicide forest, do it with Ambien! It's the easy way to erase the pain of living!"

*Painless* is *specifically designed* to appeal to adults globally. Marketing tie-ins are *specifically designed* into the product. Three examples are as follows:

1. Automotive manufacturers Cadillac and Jaguar

   Jocelyn and Aug have sex in a Cadillac. Jocelyn sells Jaguars for a living. Sure, the model years are ten-plus years out of date, but the ad campaigns can reflect that they have upgraded.

2. State of Florida tourism

   Aug and Jocelyn are in Port Everglades, Cocoa / Cocoa Beach / Cape Canaveral, Hollywood, Ponte Vedra, Palm Coast, and San Destin / Destin. Global campaigns to visit specific locations or to visit the Sunshine State can be created.

3. Alcohol marketing

   Aug orders Long Island ice teas at Poseidon's, but he can just as easily order brand $X$ Long Island iced teas. At the Bonefish Grill (another restaurant marketing opportunity), giant beers are ordered, but these could just as easily be brand $Y$ beers. These scenes can be isolated in separate marketing campaigns for the alcoholic products.

The beauty of these alcohol marketing opportunities is that the use of the products is *specifically designed* into the construct of the story so that it doesn't look like an ad. For example, in *Tomorrow Land*, halfway through the movie, everyone stops— the whole dang movie stops—and the characters all have a Coke. It's blatant and cheesy and interrupts the whole movie flow. The other thing that is stopped is the suspension of disbelief because the audience knows that the only reason for the actors doing what they are doing is to sell Coke. Ask yourself this question: Do you *pay money* to go to the movie to see a story or to watch a product placement ad?

There are other tie-ins *specifically designed* into the *Painless* product. The point is that Corporation X knows the audience being marketed to and what products are being marketed to them.

# 5. Conclusion

It doesn't matter whether a movie has a small or big budget, is independent or in a major studio, or has/doesn't have a well-known cast and crew. If the script sucks and the dialogue sucks, then the audience will *not* go pay for the product. It really is that simple!

*Painless,* the Less trilogy, and the other Poje products are *specifically designed* to have a solid script and realistic dialogue. The Corporation X senior management knows what is being created, who it is being created for, and how to market the products so that the public spends money on the products!

The two essays plus other articles sent besides have shown that there are plenty of very experienced people in the movie industry who are continuing to lose hundreds of millions of dollars annually via bad decisions being made. Their failures create a huge market void that Corporation X aims to exploit.

It's up to the reader to decide who they think knows more about using ultimately a $75 million production investment to create a movie to generate a minimum of $300 million global box office and potentially much greater global box office. The people green-lighting and creating products such as *The Sea of Trees* and *Ben-Hur* and the other financial flops documented or the people who have the *Painless* product (and more products) ready to go?

## I. *Essay no. 3: A comparison of the planned* Painless *production to the production of* The Revenant

*The Revenant* recently won two major Oscars and was nominated for many other awards. How does *Painless* stack up against *The Revenant*?

As of the time of this writing, *The Revenant* has achieved a global box office of $430 million (see this Numbers' *Revenant* link: http://www.the-numbers.com/movie/Revenant-The-(2015)#tab=summary). The box office run is nearing completion, so the current box office value can be expected to be stable. So assuming, the minimum goal of *Painless* is a global box office of $400 million and the actual intent is to be well over $500 million. The plan is for *Painless* to be a bigger smash than *The Revenant*.

The Numbers website also informs that *The Revenant* had a budget of $135 million. *Painless* is currently projected to be $75 million. This means that *Painless* costs are currently budgeted to be 55 percent of *The Revenant*. However, *The Revenant* budget undoubtedly contains two major costs that *Painless* does not have:

a. An executive producer's fee
b. Screenwriter's fee

The Hollywood Reporter and Wikipedia links below note that the original budget was $60 million and that the budget more than doubled due to rising costs. Rising costs occurred because there were many screenplay rewrites, which means that there was no clear production vision at the very beginning.

http://www.hollywoodreporter.com/news/revenant-producers-alejandro-g-inarritu-834442

https://en.wikipedia.org/wiki/The_Revenant_(2015_film)

The *Revenant* can be contrasted with the timing schedule for *Painless*, the movie, shown on page 97. The timing schedule shows how *Painless* is constructed to be a two-and-a-half-hour movie. *The Revenant* runtime is 156 minutes or 2 hours and 36 minutes on a par with *Painless* projections. Also, because the timing schedule for *Painless* exists, then there is a forum for educating all cast and crew members from day 1 of the vision and timing of *Painless*. This minimizes cost issues while allowing for clear interaction with the cast and crew to help the cast and crew maximize production value.

Ultimately, though, the product must entertain to draw a global box office of men and women. The issue comes down to "Why does *The Revenant* top out at a $430 million global box office?" The film has star power and studio resources and major Oscars. What keeps the global box office from escalating?

The answers is in the product design itself. *The Revenant* is a brutal movie featuring an attack/rape by a bear complete with maggots being used to cleanse wounds. Raw bison liver is eaten; blood pours from the character's throat as he drinks water. These design features make for an intense survival movie, but an intense survival movie caps the global box office potential because the repeat male and female is negated by the movie content.

## J. *Essay no. 4: The author's IMDB review of the movie* Elysium

The author doesn't get to the movie theater very often. Taking care of an elderly parent prevents that from occurring. However, there was one opening weekend review written and posted on IMDB. This was a review of the movie *Elysium*. The review is an IMDB website page 1 review for the movie, and the website states that 372 of 652 people found the review helpful. This makes the author one for one for creating a movie review that people enjoyed reading.

The point of including the review is that the review once again reflects that the author has a much-better grasp of what people want in a movie versus what they are getting in movies such as *Elysium*. The review is also entertainment for the reader!

## El-Stupid-ium
### poj-man (August 16, 2013)

Wow! This movie is just awful. They call it science fiction, but there is no science in it, only really bad fiction.

Have you ever noticed in these kind of futuristic society stories, they never really explain how society got to the current state it is in at the start of the movie? There is a reason why. There is no possible way that such a stupid societal construct could ever come to be! So like a Paul Krugman economic theory, the answer is that the construct exists because the premise starts out saying, "Let's assume that all logic and common sense goes out the door."(!)

Evidently, in the future, only future Los Angeles and Elysium exist. Supposedly, the world is ravaged by population and disease, but there are no Asians or EEU or South American or African members or even Washington, DC, involved with Elysium! Every politically system globally just somehow up and vanished! D'oh! So Elysium is built and lived on evidently by only Hollywood types who rule the planet! The internet, as we know it, has also completely vanished. So has email and cell phone technology, but you can still get a good deal on GMC vehicles that look like leftover Road Warrior vehicles!

Matt Damon (say it Team America–like) works in a factory where he, I guess, builds robots (?). That's a little unclear. But he is stupidly badgered into some sort of elevator-style, heat-treatment booth by his superior. Since there is no OSHA anymore, his character gets trapped in the room where they (get this!) dose the robots with human killing radiation! Now there's like no big signs up anywhere in this factory that say "Warning: Radiation at Work!" It is never explained why robots need radiation treatment, but that is what they do. And (get this!) when the treatment is done, the radiation "magically" disappears! People just walk in and out of the room! Like, WTF! How does radiation magically dissipate or get moved out of a room? It doesn't! Unless all science goes out the window!

Poor Matt. Now he has 4 days to live because of radiation poisoning, and he is very ill and can barely walk or stay awake or keep from puking for about 5 minutes! The rest of the movie, he is hooked up to a biometrically controlled exoskeleton. Matt never shows any effects of radiation poisoning, and he fights his way all over LA and Elysium! So in a complete *Johnny Mnemonic* rip-off (they should sue), Matt Damon has the magic data in his skull, and people want his head. How this all comes about is so incredibly, ridiculously stupid and unbelievable I wanted to throw things at the screen.

Matt then shows up with a grenade with the pin pulled out and his hand holding the grenade from exploding, and he demands a ride to Elysium or he will blow his head off. So not strapped in and with no refueling of any sort at all, the ship just flies off on a twelve-minute flight to Elysium! So they are breaking through Earth's atmosphere with the super rocket-powered ship. He is not strapped in and is holding a grenade, and there is no bleeping G-force causing any issues!

The final evil guy / good guy fight is just awful. The evil guy basically runs around, saying, "I could kill you, but I will continue to spout stupid statements to drag this out until you and, this will be such a surprise, manage to overcome and defeat me because I kept just spouting off the mouth rather than just killing you!"

This is after Matt goes to the armory and rescues the girly and leukemia-ridden daughter (tug my bleeding heartstrings). Now dig this, 3 bad guys are taking over Elysium. There is a big armory with plenty of weapons, and no one is coming to grab the weapons and to stop the 3-man coup of Elysium! D'oh!

To call this a craptacular is an insult to crap. This is just big-money, lazy story writing pushing a phony agenda. And it is just awful. 372 out of 652 found this helpful.

# Marketing Windup

Some readers probably are saying, "This doesn't cover all marketing! There is advertising, distribution, tie-ins, etc. to be addressed!"

Systems are already in existence that will handle those aspects of marketing. Once the second market test results come in, the corporations that have those distribution channels will want to talk. Corporations can't make money on the deal if they aren't in on the deal.

# CHAPTER 3

# Operations Plan

PRODUCING *PAINLESS* AS described in this text will require between 800 and 1,200 credited cast and crew. Most will be contract workers.

How is the estimated head count arrived at? It's by reviewing recent movie head counts on IMDB. These head counts are detailed on pages 175 to 186.

The details for each department are known. For example, *Batman v Superman* has 875 visual effects credits. Of the 875 credits, there are 69 compositors and 53 digital compositors, as well as 304 other visual effects line item jobs credited.

The *who, what, where,* and *how* of all the credited people needed gets defined by going through the timing schedule. As already noted, everything necessary to produce the film can be contracted out. The question then is whether to purchase physical assets and, if so, where, what, when, and how?

The answers to these questions are part of a general business evolution. By the time it comes around to making those specific decisions, there are more people/corporations involved. Making those decisions is nothing more than the normal course of business.

| THE MATRIX | | | THE MATRIX RELOADED | | |
| --- | --- | --- | --- | --- | --- |
| GLOBAL BOX OFFICE | | | GLOBAL BOX OFFICE | | |
| $463,517,383 | | | $738,576,929 | | |
| BUDGET | | | BUDGET | | VARIANCE |
| $65,000,000 | | | $150,000,000 | | |
| TOTAL COUNT | | 581 | TOTAL COUNT | | 1527 | 946 |

| CATEGORY | TOTAL COUNT | CATEGORY | TOTAL COUNT | |
| --- | --- | --- | --- | --- |
| DIRECTOR | 2 | DIRECTOR | 2 | 0 |
| WRITERS | 2 | WRITERS | 2 | 0 |
| CREDITED CAST | 38 | CREDITED CAST | 78 | 40 |
| UNCREDITED CAST | 0 | UNCREDITED CAST | 0 | 0 |
| PRODUCED BY | 10 | PRODUCED BY | 10 | 0 |
| MUSIC | 1 | MUSIC | 1 | 0 |
| CINEMATOGRAPHY | 1 | CINEMATOGRAPHY | 1 | 0 |
| FILM EDITING | 1 | FILM EDITING | 1 | 0 |
| CASTING | 2 | CASTING | 1 | (1) |
| PRODUCTION DESIGN | 1 | PRODUCTION DESIGN | 1 | 0 |
| ART DIRECTION | 2 | ART DIRECTION | 2 | 0 |
| SET DECORATION | 3 | SET DECORATION | 0 | (3) |
| COSTUME DESIGN | 1 | COSTUME DESIGN | 1 | 0 |
| MAKEUP DEPARTMENT | 14 | MAKEUP DEPARTMENT | 32 | 18 |
| PRODUCTION MANAGEMENT | 6 | PRODUCTION MANAGEMENT | 14 | 8 |
| SECOND UNIT DIRECTOR | 7 | SECOND UNIT DIRECTOR | 23 | 16 |
| OR ASSISTANT DIRECTOR | 0 | OR ASSISTANT DIRECTOR | 0 | 0 |
| ART DEPARTMENT | 50 | ART DEPARTMENT | 145 | 95 |
| SOUND DEPARTMENT | 25 | SOUND DEPARTMENT | 50 | 25 |
| SPECIAL EFFECTS | 53 | SPECIAL EFFECTS | 54 | 1 |
| VISUAL EFFECTS | 132 | VISUAL EFFECTS | 540 | 408 |
| STUNTS | 47 | STUNTS | 148 | 101 |
| CAMERA AND ELECTRICAL | 44 | CAMERA AND ELECTRICAL | 138 | 94 |
| ANIMATION DEPARTMENT | 1 | ANIMATION DEPARTMENT | 8 | 7 |

THE BYZANTINE PINEAPPLE (PART 1) WITH CORPORATION X ～175～

| | | |
|---|---|---|
| CASTING DEPARTMENT | 2 | |
| COSTUME AND WARDROBE | 14 | |
| EDITORIAL DEPARTMENT | 11 | |
| LOCATION MANAGEMENT | 3 | |
| MUSIC DEPARTMENT | 13 | |
| TRANSPORTATION DEPARTMENT | 3 | |
| OTHER CREW | 92 | |

| | | | |
|---|---|---|---|
| CASTING DEPARTMENT | 9 | 7 | |
| COSTUME AND WARDROBE | 28 | 14 | |
| EDITORIAL DEPARTMENT | 14 | 3 | |
| LOCATION MANAGEMENT | 12 | 9 | |
| MUSIC DEPARTMENT | 26 | 13 | |
| TRANSPORTATION DEPARTMENT | 14 | 11 | |
| OTHER CREW | 172 | 80 | |

*THE MATRIX REVOLUTIONS*

GLOBAL BOX OFFICE

$427,300,260

BUDGET

$150,000,000

TOTAL COUNT

1309

*STAR TREK BEYOND*

GLOBAL BOX OFFICE

$243,491,338

BUDGET

$185,000,000

TOTAL COUNT

1372

63

| CATEGORY | TOTAL COUNT | CATEGORY | TOTAL COUNT | |
|---|---|---|---|---|
| DIRECTOR | 2 | DIRECTOR | 1 | (1) |
| WRITERS | 2 | WRITERS | 5 | 3 |
| CREDITED CAST | 48 | CREDITED CAST | 76 | 28 |
| UNCREDITED CAST | 1 | UNCREDITED CAST | 0 | (1) |
| PRODUCED BY | 10 | PRODUCED BY | 9 | (1) |
| MUSIC | 1 | MUSIC | 1 | 0 |
| CINEMATOGRAPHY | 1 | CINEMATOGRAPHY | 1 | 0 |
| FILM EDITING | 1 | FILM EDITING | 4 | 3 |
| CASTING | 1 | CASTING | 3 | 2 |
| PRODUCTION DESIGN | 1 | PRODUCTION DESIGN | 1 | 0 |
| ART DIRECTION | 3 | ART DIRECTION | 10 | 7 |
| SET DECORATION | 0 | SET DECORATION | 2 | 2 |
| COSTUME DESIGN | 1 | COSTUME DESIGN | 1 | 0 |
| MAKEUP DEPARTMENT | 24 | MAKEUP DEPARTMENT | 34 | 10 |
| PRODUCTION MANAGEMENT | 14 | PRODUCTION MANAGEMENT | 8 | (6) |

BILL POJE

| Category | Count | Category | Count | Difference |
|---|---|---|---|---|
| SECOND UNIT DIRECTOR | 15 | SECOND UNIT DIRECTOR | 21 | 6 |
| OR ASSISTANT DIRECTOR | 0 | OR ASSISTANT DIRECTOR | 0 | 0 |
| ART DEPARTMENT | 98 | ART DEPARTMENT | 113 | 15 |
| SOUND DEPARTMENT | 47 | SOUND DEPARTMENT | 22 | (25) |
| SPECIAL EFFECTS | 41 | SPECIAL EFFECTS | 23 | (18) |
| VISUAL EFFECTS | 629 | VISUAL EFFECTS | 703 | 74 |
| STUNTS | 77 | STUNTS | 40 | (37) |
| CAMERA AND ELECTRICAL | 79 | CAMERA AND ELECTRICAL | 85 | 6 |
| ANIMATION DEPARTMENT | 14 | ANIMATION DEPARTMENT | 20 | 6 |
| CASTING DEPARTMENT | 7 | CASTING DEPARTMENT | 7 | 0 |
| COSTUME AND WARDROBE | 19 | COSTUME AND WARDROBE | 39 | 20 |
| EDITORIAL DEPARTMENT | 17 | EDITORIAL DEPARTMENT | 17 | 0 |
| LOCATION MANAGEMENT | 11 | LOCATION MANAGEMENT | 10 | (1) |
| MUSIC DEPARTMENT | 21 | MUSIC DEPARTMENT | 17 | (4) |
| TRANSPORTATION DEPARTMENT | 9 | TRANSPORTATION DEPARTMENT | 13 | 4 |
| OTHER CREW | 115 | OTHER CREW | 82 | (33) |

| *AVENGERS: AGE OF ULTRON* | | *JASON BOURNE* | | |
|---|---|---|---|---|
| GLOBAL BOX OFFICE | | GLOBAL BOX OFFICE | | |
| $1,863,711,736 | | $348,775,820 | | |
| BUDGET | | BUDGET | | |
| $250,000,000 | | $120,000,000 | | |

| TOTAL COUNT | | TOTAL COUNT | | |
|---|---|---|---|---|
| | 3402 | | 1117 | (2285) |

| CATEGORY | TOTAL COUNT | CATEGORY | TOTAL COUNT | |
|---|---|---|---|---|
| DIRECTOR | 1 | DIRECTOR | 1 | 0 |
| WRITERS | 1 | WRITERS | 2 | 1 |
| CREDITED CAST | 67 | CREDITED CAST | 42 | (25) |
| UNCREDITED CAST | 66 | UNCREDITED CAST | 164 | 98 |
| PRODUCED BY | 16 | PRODUCED BY | 13 | (3) |
| MUSIC | 2 | MUSIC | 2 | 0 |

| Department | Value | Department | Value | Change |
|---|---|---|---|---|
| CINEMATOGRAPHY | 1 | CINEMATOGRAPHY | 1 | 0 |
| FILM EDITING | 2 | FILM EDITING | 1 | (1) |
| CASTING | 2 | CASTING | 2 | 0 |
| PRODUCTION DESIGN | 1 | PRODUCTION DESIGN | 1 | 0 |
| ART DIRECTION | 8 | ART DIRECTION | 10 | 2 |
| SET DECORATION | 3 | SET DECORATION | 3 | 0 |
| COSTUME DESIGN | 1 | COSTUME DESIGN | 1 | 0 |
| MAKEUP DEPARTMENT | 108 | MAKEUP DEPARTMENT | 16 | (92) |
| PRODUCTION MANAGEMENT | 29 | PRODUCTION MANAGEMENT | 13 | (16) |
| SECOND UNIT DIRECTOR | 31 | SECOND UNIT DIRECTOR | 41 | 10 |
| OR ASSISTANT DIRECTOR | 0 | OR ASSISTANT DIRECTOR | 0 | 0 |
| ART DEPARTMENT | 190 | ART DEPARTMENT | 75 | (115) |
| SOUND DEPARTMENT | 48 | SOUND DEPARTMENT | 42 | (6) |
| SPECIAL EFFECTS | 72 | SPECIAL EFFECTS | 5 | (67) |
| VISUAL EFFECTS | 1701 | VISUAL EFFECTS | 127 | (1574) |
| STUNTS | 243 | STUNTS | 108 | (135) |
| CAMERA AND ELECTRICAL | 169 | CAMERA AND ELECTRICAL | 129 | (40) |
| ANIMATION DEPARTMENT | 57 | ANIMATION DEPARTMENT | 1 | (56) |
| CASTING DEPARTMENT | 10 | CASTING DEPARTMENT | 13 | 3 |
| COSTUME AND WARDROBE | 84 | COSTUME AND WARDROBE | 37 | (47) |
| EDITORIAL DEPARTMENT | 47 | EDITORIAL DEPARTMENT | 27 | (20) |
| LOCATION MANAGEMENT | 42 | LOCATION MANAGEMENT | 32 | (10) |
| MUSIC DEPARTMENT | 63 | MUSIC DEPARTMENT | 26 | (37) |
| TRANSPORTATION DEPARTMENT | 47 | TRANSPORTATION DEPARTMENT | 27 | (20) |
| OTHER CREW | 285 | OTHER CREW | 153 | (132) |

BILL POJE

| THE MUMMY (1999) | | THE MUMMY RETURNS | | |
|---|---|---|---|---|
| GLOBAL BOX OFFICE | | GLOBAL BOX OFFICE | | |
| $416,385,488 | | $435,040,395 | | |
| BUDGET | | BUDGET | | |
| $80,000,000 | | $98,000,000 | | |

| TOTAL COUNT | | TOTAL COUNT | | |
|---|---|---|---|---|
| | 761 | | 676 | (85) |

| CATEGORY | TOTAL COUNT | CATEGORY | TOTAL COUNT | |
|---|---|---|---|---|
| DIRECTOR | 1 | DIRECTOR | 1 | 0 |
| WRITERS | 3 | WRITERS | 1 | (2) |
| CREDITED CAST | 25 | CREDITED CAST | 18 | (7) |
| UNCREDITED CAST | 8 | UNCREDITED CAST | 6 | (2) |
| PRODUCED BY | 5 | PRODUCED BY | 5 | 0 |
| MUSIC | 1 | MUSIC | 1 | 0 |
| CINEMATOGRAPHY | 1 | CINEMATOGRAPHY | 1 | 0 |
| FILM EDITING | 1 | FILM EDITING | 2 | 1 |
| CASTING | 2 | CASTING | 2 | 0 |
| PRODUCTION DESIGN | 1 | PRODUCTION DESIGN | 1 | 0 |
| ART DIRECTION | 4 | ART DIRECTION | 3 | (1) |
| SET DECORATION | 1 | SET DECORATION | 1 | 0 |
| COSTUME DESIGN | 1 | COSTUME DESIGN | 1 | 0 |
| MAKEUP DEPARTMENT | 15 | MAKEUP DEPARTMENT | 23 | 8 |
| PRODUCTION MANAGEMENT | 7 | PRODUCTION MANAGEMENT | 12 | 5 |
| SECOND UNIT DIRECTOR | 13 | SECOND UNIT DIRECTOR | 16 | 3 |
| OR ASSISTANT DIRECTOR | 0 | OR ASSISTANT DIRECTOR | 0 | 0 |
| ART DEPARTMENT | 65 | ART DEPARTMENT | 51 | (14) |
| SOUND DEPARTMENT | 32 | SOUND DEPARTMENT | 29 | (3) |
| SPECIAL EFFECTS | 41 | SPECIAL EFFECTS | 36 | (5) |
| VISUAL EFFECTS | 221 | VISUAL EFFECTS | 202 | (19) |
| STUNTS | 85 | STUNTS | 83 | (2) |
| CAMERA AND ELECTRICAL | 61 | CAMERA AND ELECTRICAL | 56 | (5) |
| ANIMATION DEPARTMENT | 0 | ANIMATION DEPARTMENT | 6 | 6 |
| CASTING DEPARTMENT | 2 | CASTING DEPARTMENT | 6 | 4 |

| CATEGORY | THE REVENANT | SALT | DIFF |
|---|---|---|---|
| COSTUME AND WARDROBE | 14 | 11 | (3) |
| EDITORIAL / EDITORIAL DEPARTMENT | 15 | 13 | (2) |
| LOCATION MANAGEMENT | 8 | 10 | 2 |
| MUSIC DEPARTMENT | 31 | 17 | (14) |
| TRANSPORTATION DEPARTMENT | 10 | 6 | (4) |
| OTHER CREW | 82 | 51 | (31) |

|  | THE REVENANT | SALT | |
|---|---|---|---|
| GLOBAL BOX OFFICE | $532,037,894 | $290,650,494 | |
| BUDGET | $135,000,000 | $130,000,000 | |
| TOTAL COUNT | 1292 | 1184 | (108) |

| CATEGORY | TOTAL COUNT (THE REVENANT) | TOTAL COUNT (SALT) | DIFF |
|---|---|---|---|
| DIRECTOR | 1 | 1 | 0 |
| WRITERS | 2 | 1 | (1) |
| CREDITED CAST | 54 | 64 | 10 |
| UNCREDITED CAST | 15 | 97 | 82 |
| PRODUCED BY | 18 | 8 | (10) |
| MUSIC | 2 | 1 | (1) |
| CINEMATOGRAPHY | 1 | 1 | 0 |
| FILM EDITING | 1 | 2 | 1 |
| CASTING | 1 | 1 | 0 |
| PRODUCTION DESIGN | 1 | 1 | 0 |
| ART DIRECTION | 3 | 1 | (2) |
| SET DECORATION | 2 | 1 | (1) |
| COSTUME DESIGN | 1 | 1 | 0 |
| MAKEUP DEPARTMENT | 43 | 21 | (22) |
| PRODUCTION MANAGEMENT | 13 | 4 | (9) |
| SECOND UNIT DIRECTOR | 22 | 24 | 2 |
| OR ASSISTANT DIRECTOR | 0 | 0 | 0 |

BILL POJE

| CATEGORY | TOTAL COUNT | CATEGORY | TOTAL COUNT | |
|---|---|---|---|---|
| ART DEPARTMENT | 76 | ART DEPARTMENT | 94 | 18 |
| SOUND DEPARTMENT | 73 | SOUND DEPARTMENT | 46 | (27) |
| SPECIAL EFFECTS | 40 | SPECIAL EFFECTS | 23 | (17) |
| VISUAL EFFECTS | 412 | VISUAL EFFECTS | 235 | (177) |
| STUNTS | 64 | STUNTS | 119 | 55 |
| CAMERA AND ELECTRICAL | 91 | CAMERA AND ELECTRICAL | 139 | 48 |
| ANIMATION DEPARTMENT | 6 | ANIMATION DEPARTMENT | 2 | (4) |
| CASTING DEPARTMENT | 20 | CASTING DEPARTMENT | 10 | (10) |
| COSTUME AND WARDROBE | 47 | COSTUME AND WARDROBE | 22 | (25) |
| EDITORIAL DEPARTMENT | 41 | EDITORIAL DEPARTMENT | 27 | (14) |
| LOCATION MANAGEMENT | 18 | LOCATION MANAGEMENT | 30 | 12 |
| MUSIC DEPARTMENT | 23 | MUSIC DEPARTMENT | 24 | 1 |
| TRANSPORTATION DEPARTMENT | 33 | TRANSPORTATION DEPARTMENT | 8 | (25) |
| OTHER CREW | 157 | OTHER CREW | 175 | 18 |

| *SHUTTER ISLAND* | | *BATMAN VERSUS SUPERMAN* | | |
|---|---|---|---|---|
| GLOBAL BOX OFFICE | | GLOBAL BOX OFFICE | | |
| $299,461,782 | | $868,160,194 | | |
| BUDGET | | BUDGET | | |
| $80,000,000 | | $250,000,000 | | |
| TOTAL COUNT | 1051 | TOTAL COUNT | 2261 | 1210 |
| CATEGORY | TOTAL COUNT | CATEGORY | TOTAL COUNT | |
| DIRECTOR | 1 | DIRECTOR | 1 | 0 |
| WRITERS | 1 | WRITERS | 2 | 1 |
| CREDITED CAST | 161 | CREDITED CAST | 161 | 0 |
| UNCREDITED CAST | 165 | UNCREDITED CAST | 165 | 0 |
| PRODUCED BY | 12 | PRODUCED BY | 16 | 4 |
| MUSIC | 0 | MUSIC | 2 | 2 |
| CINEMATOGRAPHY | 1 | CINEMATOGRAPHY | 1 | 0 |
| FILM EDITING | 1 | FILM EDITING | 1 | 0 |
| CASTING | 1 | CASTING | 3 | 2 |

| CATEGORY | COUNT | CATEGORY | TOTAL COUNT | |
|---|---|---|---|---|
| PRODUCTION DESIGN | 1 | PRODUCTION DESIGN | 1 | 0 |
| ART DIRECTION | 3 | ART DIRECTION | 6 | 3 |
| SET DECORATION | 1 | SET DECORATION | 1 | 0 |
| COSTUME DESIGN | 1 | COSTUME DESIGN | 1 | 0 |
| MAKEUP DEPARTMENT | 19 | MAKEUP DEPARTMENT | 37 | 18 |
| PRODUCTION MANAGEMENT | 4 | PRODUCTION MANAGEMENT | 10 | 6 |
| SECOND UNIT DIRECTOR | 8 | SECOND UNIT DIRECTOR | 14 | 6 |
| OR ASSISTANT DIRECTOR | 0 | OR ASSISTANT DIRECTOR | 0 | 0 |
| ART DEPARTMENT | 187 | ART DEPARTMENT | 133 | (54) |
| SOUND DEPARTMENT | 29 | SOUND DEPARTMENT | 29 | 0 |
| SPECIAL EFFECTS | 37 | SPECIAL EFFECTS | 37 | 0 |
| VISUAL EFFECTS | 95 | VISUAL EFFECTS | 875 | 780 |
| STUNTS | 16 | STUNTS | 118 | 102 |
| CAMERA AND ELECTRICAL | 94 | CAMERA AND ELECTRICAL | 138 | 44 |
| ANIMATION DEPARTMENT | 0 | ANIMATION DEPARTMENT | 24 | 24 |
| CASTING DEPARTMENT | 8 | CASTING DEPARTMENT | 19 | 11 |
| COSTUME AND WARDROBE | 17 | COSTUME AND WARDROBE | 55 | 38 |
| EDITORIAL DEPARTMENT | 14 | EDITORIAL DEPARTMENT | 32 | 18 |
| LOCATION MANAGEMENT | 10 | LOCATION MANAGEMENT | 28 | 18 |
| MUSIC DEPARTMENT | 5 | MUSIC DEPARTMENT | 52 | 47 |
| TRANSPORTATION DEPARTMENT | 12 | TRANSPORTATION DEPARTMENT | 45 | 33 |
| OTHER CREW | 147 | OTHER CREW | 225 | 78 |

| *SUICIDE SQUAD* | | *INCEPTION* | | |
|---|---|---|---|---|
| GLOBAL BOX OFFICE | | GLOBAL BOX OFFICE | | |
| $638,562,545 | | $832,584,416 | | |
| BUDGET | | BUDGET | | |
| $175,000,000 | | $160,000,000 | | |
| TOTAL COUNT | 1420 | TOTAL COUNT | 1347 | (73) |
| CATEGORY | TOTAL COUNT | CATEGORY | TOTAL COUNT | |
| DIRECTOR | 1 | DIRECTOR | 1 | 0 |

| | | | |
|---|---|---|---|
| WRITERS | 2 | WRITERS | 1 | (1) |
| CREDITED CAST | 126 | CREDITED CAST | 78 | (48) |
| UNCREDITED CAST | 0 | UNCREDITED CAST | 0 | 0 |
| PRODUCED BY | 10 | PRODUCED BY | 10 | 0 |
| MUSIC | 1 | MUSIC | 1 | 0 |
| CINEMATOGRAPHY | 1 | CINEMATOGRAPHY | 1 | 0 |
| FILM EDITING | 1 | FILM EDITING | 1 | 0 |
| CASTING | 1 | CASTING | 1 | 0 |
| PRODUCTION DESIGN | 1 | PRODUCTION DESIGN | 1 | 0 |
| ART DIRECTION | 6 | ART DIRECTION | 3 | (3) |
| SET DECORATION | 2 | SET DECORATION | 2 | 0 |
| COSTUME DESIGN | 1 | COSTUME DESIGN | 1 | 0 |
| MAKEUP DEPARTMENT | 43 | MAKEUP DEPARTMENT | 27 | (16) |
| PRODUCTION MANAGEMENT | 6 | PRODUCTION MANAGEMENT | 13 | 7 |
| SECOND UNIT DIRECTOR OR ASSISTANT DIRECTOR | 38 0 | SECOND UNIT DIRECTOR OR ASSISTANT DIRECTOR | 27 0 | (11) 0 |
| ART DEPARTMENT | 111 | ART DEPARTMENT | 157 | 46 |
| SOUND DEPARTMENT | 34 | SOUND DEPARTMENT | 37 | 3 |
| SPECIAL EFFECTS | 24 | SPECIAL EFFECTS | 61 | 37 |
| VISUAL EFFECTS | 457 | VISUAL EFFECTS | 268 | (189) |
| STUNTS | 118 | STUNTS | 102 | (16) |
| CAMERA AND ELECTRICAL | 122 | CAMERA AND ELECTRICAL | 142 | 20 |
| ANIMATION DEPARTMENT | 16 | ANIMATION DEPARTMENT | 0 | (16) |
| CASTING DEPARTMENT | 9 | CASTING DEPARTMENT | 13 | 4 |
| COSTUME AND WARDROBE | 54 | COSTUME AND WARDROBE | 42 | (12) |
| EDITORIAL DEPARTMENT | 24 | EDITORIAL DEPARTMENT | 28 | 4 |
| LOCATION MANAGEMENT | 8 | LOCATION MANAGEMENT | 38 | 30 |
| MUSIC DEPARTMENT | 41 | MUSIC DEPARTMENT | 45 | 4 |
| TRANSPORTATION DEPARTMENT | 20 | TRANSPORTATION DEPARTMENT | 42 | 22 |
| OTHER CREW | 139 | OTHER CREW | 202 | 63 |

| ALICE THROUGH THE LOOKING GLASS | | | GHOSTBUSTERS (2016) | | |
|---|---|---|---|---|---|
| GLOBAL BOX OFFICE | | | GLOBAL BOX OFFICE | | |
| $277,439,494 | | | $217,748,707 | | |
| BUDGET | | | BUDGET | | |
| $170,000,000 | | | $144,000,000 | | |
| TOTAL COUNT | | | TOTAL COUNT | | |
| | | 1392 | | 1422 | 30 |
| CATEGORY | TOTAL COUNT | | CATEGORY | TOTAL COUNT | |
| DIRECTOR | 1 | | DIRECTOR | 1 | 0 |
| WRITERS | 1 | | WRITERS | 2 | 1 |
| CREDITED CAST | 83 | | CREDITED CAST | 55 | (28) |
| UNCREDITED CAST | 0 | | UNCREDITED CAST | 135 | 135 |
| PRODUCED BY | 8 | | PRODUCED BY | 14 | 6 |
| MUSIC | 1 | | MUSIC | 1 | 0 |
| CINEMATOGRAPHY | 1 | | CINEMATOGRAPHY | 1 | 0 |
| FILM EDITING | 1 | | FILM EDITING | 2 | 1 |
| CASTING | 2 | | CASTING | 0 | (2) |
| PRODUCTION DESIGN | 1 | | PRODUCTION DESIGN | 1 | 0 |
| ART DIRECTION | 6 | | ART DIRECTION | 5 | (1) |
| SET DECORATION | 2 | | SET DECORATION | 1 | (1) |
| COSTUME DESIGN | 1 | | COSTUME DESIGN | 1 | 0 |
| MAKEUP DEPARTMENT | 31 | | MAKEUP DEPARTMENT | 18 | (13) |
| PRODUCTION MANAGEMENT | 10 | | PRODUCTION MANAGEMENT | 7 | (3) |
| SECOND UNIT DIRECTOR | 14 | | SECOND UNIT DIRECTOR | 13 | (1) |
| OR ASSISTANT DIRECTOR | 0 | | OR ASSISTANT DIRECTOR | 0 | 0 |
| ART DEPARTMENT | 148 | | ART DEPARTMENT | 118 | (30) |
| SOUND DEPARTMENT | 29 | | SOUND DEPARTMENT | 37 | 8 |
| SPECIAL EFFECTS | 33 | | SPECIAL EFFECTS | 33 | 0 |
| VISUAL EFFECTS | 654 | | VISUAL EFFECTS | 485 | (169) |
| STUNTS | 23 | | STUNTS | 85 | 62 |
| CAMERA AND ELECTRICAL | 81 | | CAMERA AND ELECTRICAL | 113 | 32 |
| ANIMATION DEPARTMENT | 32 | | ANIMATION DEPARTMENT | 28 | (4) |

BILL POJE

| CATEGORY | COUNT | CATEGORY | COUNT | DIFF |
|---|---|---|---|---|
| CASTING DEPARTMENT | 3 | CASTING DEPARTMENT | 11 | 8 |
| COSTUME AND WARDROBE | 35 | COSTUME AND WARDROBE | 45 | 10 |
| EDITORIAL DEPARTMENT | 28 | EDITORIAL DEPARTMENT | 12 | (16) |
| LOCATION MANAGEMENT | 9 | LOCATION MANAGEMENT | 19 | 10 |
| MUSIC DEPARTMENT | 24 | MUSIC DEPARTMENT | 35 | 11 |
| TRANSPORTATION DEPARTMENT | 15 | TRANSPORTATION DEPARTMENT | 10 | (5) |
| OTHER CREW | 112 | OTHER CREW | 132 | 20 |

| *WANTED* | | *BEN-HUR* (2016) | | |
|---|---|---|---|---|
| GLOBAL BOX OFFICE | | GLOBAL BOX OFFICE | | |
| $342,416,460 | | $41,815,925 | | |
| BUDGET | | BUDGET | | |
| $75,000,000 | | $95,000,000 | | |

| TOTAL COUNT | | TOTAL COUNT | | |
|---|---|---|---|---|
| | 1140 | | 718 | (422) |

| CATEGORY | TOTAL COUNT | CATEGORY | TOTAL COUNT | |
|---|---|---|---|---|
| DIRECTOR | 1 | DIRECTOR | 1 | 0 |
| WRITERS | 5 | WRITERS | 2 | (3) |
| CREDITED CAST | 17 | CREDITED CAST | 35 | 18 |
| UNCREDITED CAST | 18 | 0 | 0 | (18) |
| PRODUCED BY | 16 | PRODUCED BY | 10 | (6) |
| MUSIC | 1 | MUSIC | 1 | 0 |
| CINEMATOGRAPHY | 1 | CINEMATOGRAPHY | 1 | 0 |
| FILM EDITING | 1 | FILM EDITING | 3 | 2 |
| CASTING | 1 | CASTING | 1 | 0 |
| PRODUCTION DESIGN | 1 | PRODUCTION DESIGN | 1 | 0 |
| ART DIRECTION | 4 | ART DIRECTION | 7 | 3 |
| SET DECORATION | 1 | SET DECORATION | 1 | 0 |
| COSTUME DESIGN | 1 | COSTUME DESIGN | 1 | 0 |
| MAKEUP DEPARTMENT | 25 | MAKEUP DEPARTMENT | 19 | (6) |
| PRODUCTION MANAGEMENT | 7 | PRODUCTION MANAGEMENT | 12 | 5 |
| SECOND UNIT DIRECTOR | 26 | SECOND UNIT DIRECTOR | 18 | (8) |

| | | | | |
|---|---|---|---|---|
| OR ASSISTANT DIRECTOR | 0 | OR ASSISTANT DIRECTOR | 0 | 0 |
| ART DEPARTMENT | 69 | ART DEPARTMENT | 33 | (36) |
| SOUND DEPARTMENT | 40 | SOUND DEPARTMENT | 23 | (17) |
| SPECIAL EFFECTS | 66 | SPECIAL EFFECTS | 27 | (39) |
| VISUAL EFFECTS | 334 | VISUAL EFFECTS | 275 | (59) |
| STUNTS | 81 | STUNTS | 45 | (36) |
| CAMERA AND ELECTRICAL | 115 | CAMERA AND ELECTRICAL | 73 | (42) |
| ANIMATION DEPARTMENT | 3 | ANIMATION DEPARTMENT | 1 | (2) |
| CASTING DEPARTMENT | 8 | CASTING DEPARTMENT | 8 | 0 |
| COSTUME AND WARDROBE | 13 | COSTUME AND WARDROBE | 24 | 11 |
| EDITORIAL DEPARTMENT | 23 | EDITORIAL DEPARTMENT | 20 | (3) |
| LOCATION MANAGEMENT | 22 | LOCATION MANAGEMENT | 3 | (19) |
| MUSIC DEPARTMENT | 37 | MUSIC DEPARTMENT | 6 | (31) |
| TRANSPORTATION DEPARTMENT | 19 | TRANSPORTATION DEPARTMENT | 4 | (15) |
| OTHER CREW | 179 | OTHER CREW | 63 | (116) |

# CHAPTER 4

# Other Corporate Department Plan Summaries

I *NFORMATION SYSTEM PLAN*

Obviously, there is a massive amount of IT needs:

a.  Production hardware and software
b.  ERP/accounting systems
c.  Communications systems
d.  Storage systems
e.  Security systems

The author already has IT personnel lined up to start the ball rolling. The author has also installed ERP/accounting systems, biometric time and attendance systems, financial report writers, and ideated/designed/ started implementation of a database/programming to take continuous PLC data from a massive factory running 24-7-365 into the database and out to management.

Addressing the information systems needs of Corporation X is not a concern. There are plenty of capable IT personnel available to be utilized to address the IT needs of Corporation X.

## Human Resource Plan

There are three-hundred-million-plus people in the USA. Many talented people work in the entertainment industry. Many of the people welcome the opportunity to have a job on a big-budget film such as *Painless* is envisioned to be. Finding talent is not an issue.

As noted, there are one thousand or so credited people on a production such as *Painless*, as well as the people involved in marketing or other office positions. The key is establishing a management team capable of managing all the contract and direct-hire people required to pull making not only *Painless* but also establishing the teams required to create the next ten years' worth of products.

Assuming that the second market test is as successful as envisioned, the belief is that many of the staff required will be those making the twenty-five-dollar donation to get on the quarterly newsletter. Their belief will be that this will put them in a position to become involved in growing Corporation X.

Finding and managing human resources is not foreseen as a major headache. It is just standard management work.

## Legal Plan

A Beverly Hills entertainment industry law firm in Wilshire Boulevard is ready to start working on all the legal needs of Corporation X. All that is required is the funding to employ their services.

## Accounting Plan

The author is a degreed accountant who was the financial controller for the largest exporter out of the Bahamas. The author installed a full ERP/accounting system and a biometric time and attendance system, as well as a payroll system. The author handled the audits and worked with the Central Bank of the Bahamas for cash-transfer issues.

Establishing and managing the accounting and cash management system is not foreseen as a major headache. It is just standard management work.

## Finance Plan

The applicable phrase is "There are deals, and there are deals." Financing Corporation X is a matter of managing a succession of financial and legal deals. The author has never been involved in a business that didn't have continuously evolving financial deals.

The author, as a businessperson, is prepared to discuss various levels of investment, but the two primary issues are

1. funding the second market test and to what level of production effort is decided to be funded and
2. funding the fixed asset location and what that inherently means in terms of funding the production of *Painless* as the movie described in the vision.

Funding these two items inherently leads to funding the production and marketing of *Painless* as a movie, as well as producing and marketing other products. There are many ways to make a deal/deals to fund corporate expansion. There are deals, and there are deals.

# CHAPTER 5

# Conclusion

I F THE READER has made it this far, then *congratulations!* You
have completed approximately forty thousand words and a series
of charts, not to mention a brand-new macroeconomic formula! The
author would like the reader to know how appreciative of the reader he
is for having completed reading the text.

The reader will have to decide for themselves whether this text
should be classified as nonfiction or fiction. Obviously, the author
considers it nonfiction.

*The Byzantine Pineapple* lays out the concepts for prebudgeting
government while also accomplishing 100 percent coverage of all citizens
for capital to exist on housing as well as health care. Corporation X lays
out the plan for making quite literally billions of dollars while also
establishing the central command for moving forward with promotion
of *The Byzantine Pineapple* concepts. And the author accomplishes this
in 20 percent less text than the *Painless* novel! Not too shabby for a
nonindustry-experienced village idiot!

With respect to Corporation X, the author is fond of stating that
the word *management* means one of two things:

1. The situation is managed.
2. The management team somehow manages to get by.

The opinion of the author is that this text demonstrates that the
Corporate X's situation is managed.

The author is also of the opinion that this text presents a path to literally make billions of sales dollars while also work to improve the future of humans globally via the advancement of the principles laid out in *The Byzantine Pineapple*. The principles are founded in nonviolent changes to move to a system that truly does treat people as equals while allowing for more capitalistic freedom and, at the same time, providing 100 percent certainty to all citizens to have housing and medical covered and provide a bare-enough income to live off.

By sheer coincidence, the second *Rambo* movie was on in the background while the author was typing this conclusion. Considering all the failed attempts at government corruption reform, the author heard the following dialogue and felt that it was an apropos closing quote:

> Rambo: Do we get to win this time?
> Colonel Trautman: This time, it's up to you.

For the reform to take place, it is up to you to support the plan.

CPSIA information can be obtained
at www.ICGtesting.com
Printed in the USA
BVHW031632091218
534470BV00012B/56/P